This book should be returned to any branch of the
Lancashire County Library on or before the date shown

CROFT/IR
7.15
ECL

Clitheroe Library
01200 428788
7/10
B.CAP. 10/15
3 0 SEP 2010
B.GRO 12.15
4 NOV 2010
B.BUR
9 NOV 2010
14 FEB 2017
0 9 APR
G. PAR. 6/13
M.BAM. 7/13
PC 1/14
28 JAN 19
J. WHI. 5/14
CROFT/MA
- 6.14
MF/PW
5.15

D0298812

Lancashire County Libra
Bowran Street
Preston PR1 2UX
www.lanc
Lancashire County Library

Lancashire County Council

30118114442431

GROWING UP IN SUSSEX

GROWING UP IN SUSSEX

FROM SCHOOLBOY TO SOLDIER

GERRY WELLS

LARGE PRINT
Oxford

Copyright © Gerry Wells, 2009

First published in Great Britain 2009
by
The History Press

Published in Large Print 2009 by ISIS Publishing Ltd.,
7 Centremead, Osney Mead, Oxford OX2 0ES
by arrangement with
The History Press

All rights reserved

The moral right of the author has been asserted

British Library Cataloguing in Publication Data
Wells, Gerald.
    Growing up in Sussex: from schoolboy to soldier.
    - - (Reminiscence)
    1. Wells, Gerald - - Childhood and youth.
    2. Young men - - England - - Sussex - - Biography.
    3. Sussex (England) - - Social life and customs
    - - 20th century.
    4. Large type books.
    I. Title II. Series   11444243
    942.2'5082'092–dc22

ISBN 978–0–7531–9540–6 (hb)
ISBN 978–0–7531–9541–3 (pb)

Printed and bound in Great Britain by
T. J. International Ltd., Padstow, Cornwall

Dedication

For all my family – with love.

Acknowledgements

All thanks to my wife Gill, without whom this book would never have been written; her help, interest and expert proofreader's eye have been invaluable. I am indebted to Jason and Katy Ellis for the magic they worked on photographs that had been languishing in a box for the last seventy years or so. Also to Ann Foxall and Sarah Kyne at the Bexhill and Eastbourne Libraries, and Anne Drewery at Lancing College Archives. I am very grateful for the help they all provided.

Contents

CHAPTER
ONE

A Boy's Eye View

Remembering the brutal fact of my falling into the pond when I was playing with a toy boat, gave me the starting point for this memoir. It was my first experience of anything really unpleasant existing outside the warm protected life I had experienced up to that moment. The water was cold as winter and as black: I sank and thought I'd sink forever — and you don't forget moments like that. Rescued by Father, probably startled from his newspaper, I was handed dripping and yelling over the fence to be sorted out by Mother who wouldn't have been very amused. A second baptism perhaps, just to make sure.

So that was a start. Another early milestone was when my parents built a house — but this was mainly because Mr Banks, the foreman, wore a bowler hat, which makes the memory stick. That was sometime in 1930 when I was rising five, and Mr Banks, the bowler, appeared massive both in stature and importance, not only to me I suspect, because he was both hirer and firer in days when jobs were very few and far between. One memorable morning, resplendent in suit and shiny boots as well as his bowler, he handed me a trowel loaded with cement and together we rather messily laid the first brick. From that small beginning my parents acquired a four-bedroomed house with oak fitments and parquet floors, garden, garage and gravel drive for £1,800. Those were times before Monopoly money.

For me it was to be a wonderful place in which to grow up, with railway line and woods behind, cliffs and the sea a spit away in front. Before the Southern Railway system was electrified, steam engines ruled: fiery as dragons they sparked and roared on their way to and from Eastbourne and Hastings, their furnace breath firing up the embankments behind us, to burn in crackling fury with orange flame and the scented smoke of dry-as-tinder grass. Later, the primroses appeared as they always did, bright islands in a sea of fire-pungent blackness — a first indication to me of the way nature works.

Those were days of extremes. For Father earning about £500 a year in a job with prospects and Mother with a small private income, it was possible to pay for my schooling and run a car, as well as to employ Lucy our maid for £1 a week and her keep, with a half-day off on Thursday and Sunday afternoons. They must have been comfortable days for my parents with a varied social life of parties, cinema and dances, together with an occasional Thomas Cook's holiday abroad in summer.

Lucy, from a home where bread and scrape ruled, was the central figure for me: unflappable, warm, she functioned as ally, dispenser of gorgeous by-products of cooking sessions, as well as being coverer-up of all but my most awful indiscretions. The conventional side of her work meant she more than helped with the cooking, polished, dusted, and generally kept the house at the new-pin standards required by Mother. Wearing a pinafore in the mornings, she changed into a brown dress with frilly cap and apron in the afternoons, when at 4p.m. she pushed a loaded trolley into the drawing room for Mother's tea. That was when, if not at school, I sat in the kitchen with Lucy consuming large quantities of bread and jam, talking non stop with my mouth full and my elbows on the table: it was a blissful escape and we both knew it.

With Lucy, Mother ran the proverbial tight ship as far as the housekeeping was concerned — routine ruled, so you pretty well knew what would be going on at any given time. Routine also applied to our meals, which followed their seemingly immutable sequence, starting with Sunday's roast with the usual trimmings, thence to variations on that basic theme, leading to Thursday's Irish stew (the worst) plus, of course, fish on Friday. So if you'd forgotten which day it was you only had to look at what was on your plate. I was then, and still am, pretty well omnivorous except for Irish stew, rhubarb and prunes. But Thursdays were purgatory, the odorous Irish stew arriving in a deep pot always loaded with pearl barley and bits of varying size, which were either sharp fragments of bone or gelatinously squidgy and unidentifiable; the only obvious ingredient was the pearl barley which I hated — one way and another it was a bit like excavating a swamp, then having to eat it. But I carp — we were the lucky ones eating regularly and well, and I thrived on it.

Living in a very different world from us were the unemployed, of whom there were millions. In those years after the financial crash of 1929, there were few safety nets for the poor or out of work. For this reason England's roads carried a heavy traffic of tramps journeying from one Spike to the next, men permanently on the move loaded with blankets, clanking with billycans and anything else they possessed. A Spike was a council-run refuge spaced miles from the next one, and was set up to provide a meal and shelter for one night only — with no return for so many months to keep men on the move. Often they would come to our back door asking for hot water for a brew-up, men still with pride enough to ask for a job to do in exchange for what they received. Lucy would make them a sandwich if Mother wasn't there, or slip them a biscuit to go with the water if she was. Many of these men were those who had served for years in France in the First World War — survivors in fact, back in the "Land fit for heroes" that had been promised.

As a very small boy still at the hand-holding stage and wearing those tedious winter gaiters that made even Lucy tight-lipped as she battled with the button hook, I remember seeing former soldiers with medals on their frayed jackets and often with their collars turned up on cold days, standing on street corners selling matches and bootlaces from a tray slung from their necks. Sometimes a group of them would be trudging along a street gutter in single file playing whatever instruments they had — sometimes with one of them twanging a Jew's harp. I was too young to take in the hopelessness of all that, but sights like those have never left me and I drew my conclusions long ago. It was small wonder there were no recruiting difficulties in 1939 when the inevitable happened — at least you were sure of food and shelter even if they might cost you your life.

At that time much was made of each 11 November as seems to be happening again today. At 11 a.m. precisely, the town's maroon, an explosive firework, used to alert the fire brigade, was fired with a great sonorous boom, and for two minutes the whole country came to a standstill. I was with Mother in town on one occasion — all traffic stopped and we stood stock still on a draughty street corner in what seemed an endless spooky silence. On another occasion we were listening to the service at the Cenotaph on the wireless, when the silence was broken by a woman's voice calling out: "Why this hypocrisy when you're preparing for another war?" — it was so urgent and clear that I've never forgotten the drama of it, and have always hoped she was treated better than the Suffragettes had been in their day. An irony of those annual proceedings and something else I saw only much later, was that the country seemed to be paying more attention to the last war's dead than to its survivors.

A more positive aspect of life and an asset for most people, must have been the fact that the price of pretty well everything in those days changed very little over the years. Hard experience tells me you can get used to practically anything as we have to today; the price of something goes up a couple of million per cent and we shrug our shoulders, blame the politicians and pay up. But Father, used to better things, would have thought about writing to his local MP if petrol had gone up by as much as a penny or two on the 1s 3d a gallon, which it was for years, top quality too — and it would have been the same had his cigarettes gone up at all. He smoked Craven A's in their red packet with its black cat staring out from a white oval — a matter of great importance as far as I was concerned, since they were the source of a brilliant series of very swappable cigarette cards, usually cars and footballers — a currency in themselves at school. Maybe it was just expectation backed by cheap products from an Empire that kept things as they were, a fact of life that was taken for granted without any thought of change.

At a time in my life when every day seemed to come up with something new, I soaked it all up greedily; if the day was a really lucky one when we were in town, the fire maroon would go off and we might see the astounding spectacle of the fire engine in full cry to its fire. Fire engines then were magnificent machines with enormous extending ladders and polished brass just about everywhere, and the crew wearing big brass helmets, clinging on to whatever they could find — with one of them ding-dinging a big brass bell as the great red monster roared past. "It's not hard to see what they do all the time when they're not at fires", Mother would remark.

There were less dramatic things to look at too; when it got dark early on winter afternoons, the lamplighters in Bexhill were busy. There was electricity then but time switches had still to be invented, so the lamplighter with his long pole could often be seen going along the streets switching on each light as he came to it; sometimes he would be on a bicycle with a pole precariously perched on his shoulder, but he'd be so expert at the job that he'd stay on his bike, maybe wobbling a bit but never failing to get to the switch at his first attempt.

And then if I were particularly lucky, the rag-and-bone man — first heard from a distance, would come round the corner belting-out his "rag'n bones, rag'n bones" — a two-note bellow echoing up and down the street. He always sat swinging his legs from the side of a flat cart with wooden wheels, pulled by a cadaverous horse. Remember Steptoe on his rounds and you've got the picture, though as I recall the programme, his horse was prosperous by comparison and his posh cart had rubber tyres. What do you do with a cartload of rags and bones I wondered — I think the bones were for making the horrible smelly glues of the time, but I never found out what happened to the rags, though they must have had a future somewhere.

In the early 1930s milk used not to come in bottles unless you lived out of town; in Bexhill it came round in churns on a little hand cart pushed by the milkman. I suppose he would have had his call too, something like "milko" probably, though I never heard him — but I often saw the milk being ladled out: he'd dip from the churn then pour from a great height with practised aim, making the milk froth into each of his customers' cans; the ladles were of different capacities and he carried them swinging and dripping from the push handle of his cart. I'm pretty sure everybody got a lot more than just plain milk in their jugs: for a start there were few, if any, tuberculin tested herds then — and there would have been plenty of happily lurking bacteria and heaven knows what else, especially on a hot day.

When I was about six, a couple of unpleasant things happened to me; after a bout of tonsillitis with the usual high temperatures, I sprouted a squint — I just woke up with it one morning. In the end it was corrected surgically but it was something that involved having to wear glasses, which is a bind when you're young — especially at school when they're always getting broken. The plus side of this affliction meant occasional trips to London to see Mr Hudson, an ophthalmic surgeon. Apart from the excitement of travelling by steam train from what was then Bexhill's north station to Charing Cross, smelling the soot and watching telegraph poles flying rhythmically up and down past the carriage window, was Mr Hudson himself, small and seeming incredibly old, who had a fascinating clockwork singing bird in a cage on his desk. After, always after, he had finished shining lights in my eyes, he would take me on his knee and wind up the little green bird on its perch to set it singing and flapping its wings. I was always mesmerised, and on a good day he would wind it up again to repeat the performance. It was a dark and fusty smelling consulting room with heavy curtains, but that little mechanical bird really lit up the stuffy place. I recall that his fee for those consultations was five guineas and that seemed a real bargain — at least to me.

Other attractions of those trips to London very often involved going to the zoo or the waxworks at Madam Tussaud's and afterwards, treat of treats, afternoon tea with sandwiches and gorgeous sticky cakes at the Strand Palace when Father was feeling rich — or a Lyon's Corner House if he wasn't. He was a Londoner who knew the place inside and out, and he'd often take us from Mr Hudson's consulting rooms by way of a maze of byways and snickets, as he called them, emerging into the world of main streets and shops — which included an unforgettable butcher's shop with men in boaters and stained striped aprons, the place hung with bloody sides of beef that dripped disturbingly into the sawdust on the floor.

London seemed a turbulent, unsettling place of scurrying pedestrians, its streets blue with exhaust fumes from noisy motors honking at ponies and traps doing their best to dodge enormous horse-drawn drays loaded with barrels — driven by men wearing bowler hats and green-baize aprons. Then there were the trams. Those trams were fabulous, great red double-deckers plastered with their vivid "Bisto" and "Guiness" advertisements, rocking and squealing on rails set into the road — rails that Father said would quickly part cyclist from bike if he were careless enough to get his front wheel trapped. The tram driver standing importantly at the front, controlled the swaying beast by twiddling a big brass handle, I believe they were known as dead man's handles, if you let go the tram stopped, not a bad safety measure if the driver had a problem, given the size of the tram and the congestion of the streets.

On one visit as a special favour, I was allowed to stand beside the driver as we sparked and clattered along the busy streets — suddenly a cyclist leaving things a bit late, crossed close in front of us, pedalling furiously.

"I eats them bikers for breakfast" the driver remarked with a sideways look at me, "before me bacon and eggs — tasty they are." I wasn't all that sure whether it was the cyclist or the bacon and eggs that were the tasty part — but somehow the next-to-the-driver experience had palled a little for me. He was a large man with a ferocious moustache and a stomach that suggested a lifetime of tasty breakfasts. I wondered what else he might relish with such appetite, thanked him very politely and went back to my parents. I took up this bothersome matter with Father when we got off.

"That driver said he ate cyclists for breakfast" I remarked as casually as I could, "was he joking?" Thoughtfully Father sucked at a tooth. "You never know, it's probably a perk of the job — how many cyclists have you see today?"

"Just that one I think."

"Well, there you are" said Father, not quite meeting my eye, "I don't suppose there are many left — and he was probably lucky to get away with it." I half-believed that London trams had drivers who breakfasted on cyclists for nearly as long as I half-believed in Father Christmas — and on later London visits I regarded passing trams with a new respect.

CHAPTER
TWO

Summer Times

The major misfortune that struck round about that time was the assault of a burst appendix followed by peritonitis. I was about six at the time but still remember very clearly how a nagging pain in my stomach increased through the day, until at bedtime it had become a driving agony that had me screaming. Our doctor didn't take long to diagnose the problem, but by then I was away with the fairies; I vaguely remember being carried by Father to the car and being driven to a nursing home in Bexhill — those being the days before the town had a hospital. On arrival I was prepared for surgery, taken by trolley into a white room with very bright lights — and that was that for a long time until I surfaced into a twilight world of high temperatures and half-comprehended activity. It was a strange dream-drifting period — but one always with a somehow familiar background that I later recognised as being the comfortable voice of the sea, which was only 200yds from my window.

After surgery in those days you were kept in bed for ages, for many hot and uncomfortable weeks in my case — so long in fact, that I had to learn to walk again and in the process found myself watching a lot of summer slipping away. All the scenes and sounds of the world of beach — a sparkling sea, the emotive buzz of outboard motors and all the noises of children and dogs doing their things, came tantalisingly in through my open window, and that was as near as I got to any of it. It was agony.

Anyway, that was just one summer — and other summers were big in my life; for most of them I ran pretty wild, brown as a nut and heavily scarred with scratches and bruises. The main asset to running wild was my alter ego, Stanley, who lived down the road from us, and was a couple of years older than I. He wore horn-rimmed glasses, had flat feet, but was stronger, heavier, and could run faster — for a start anyway; however, I could climb higher when it came to trees and I swam more strongly — so we weren't all that ill-matched. What I most envied Stanley was the fact that he didn't live in a showroom-tidy house, and had a wonderful attic room all to himself — which was often a wet-day refuge and centre for serious fort versus fort battles, Desperate Dan — and items of food filched from his mother's store cupboard. On other occasions, wearied by our latest confrontation, there would be periods of reflection, when such important matters as the actual differences between men and women were considered, an on-going preoccupation for Stanley, who tended to worry at this conundrum like a dog at a bone — but I being somewhat younger with the sap still to rise, tended to doze off.

13

We had sea and woods on our doorsteps, with the space between our houses and the sea a scrubby prairie of gorse and impenetrable blackberry thicket, a wild place of imaginative treasure. Even now I can conjure up the scent of gorse flowers and the dried-out grasses concealing deadly snakes coiled and fanged like cobras — though we never saw any — but scared each other by saying we did. When we weren't fighting a last-ditch battle against invading Normans, we climbed and fell down cliffs that crumbled wickedly underfoot, built dens in brambly places, had fights, catapults and infinite time. We were given 6d a week pocket money, which did us pretty well: you could stop the Wall's ice-cream man on his "Stop me and buy one" tricycle and have a fruit-flavoured water ice for 1d or a choc ice for 2d when you could afford it. If you achieved the nearly impossible and saved for a couple of weeks, there was the Aladdin's cave of Mr Barker's toy shop in Bexhill to relieve you of it; we didn't have to buy our catapults except for the elastic as we were good at making the vital fork ourselves which naturally involved climbing impossible trees.

Looking back to times as far removed as those, I'm inclined to think all summers were hot and sunny. Of course they weren't, and it's not too hard to call up those wild Channel storms that rode their shingle-filled waves off the horizon to crash over the promenade where the colonnade and bandstand stood; with very high tides both were perilously close to the sea and to us a great focus of interest in bad weather. When we were older, Stanley and I would play chicken by running through the danger area between waves, risking a soaking — or worse if we didn't time it right. How we made it without being washed round the coast to Hastings, I can't tell.

But many a magical summer's day started on the beach opposite where we lived, mornings when the sea was still spooked by early fog. At high tide we had only shingle to occupy us, though beachcombing was always exciting with anything possible but when the tide was out, there lay another world of sand striated by the sea's currents and dotted with rocks and rock pools full of life. I think we were aware then of what those expeditions were giving us, though it was never articulated or fully comprehended beyond the excitement of the moment.

There was the sensuous pleasure of splashing ankle-deep along the tide-line with the sand gritty and warm oozing between our toes; we hoped in vain to find bottles with desperate messages inside them — but once found a dead dog that quivered the air with its presence, the sea's offerings being many and various. There was another magic to be found in a crystal-clear pool, the kind fringed by that special seaweed blessed with bubbles that pop when you squeeze them. You might find the orange symmetry of a live starfish trapped and waiting for the returning tide, or see a cloud of floating sand that says you've just missed a retreating crab: those pools were teeming microcosmic worlds, and they fascinated us.

One day while we were poking about among the rocks, a flying boat with one of its engines cut, came down on the sea in curtains of glittering spray to settle like a great bird a few hundred yards offshore. It was silver and fabulous with its red, white and blue markings and a wealth of struts and wires between its wings. We sat on a rock gawping as a figure appeared from the cabin and began to tinker with one of the engines. What he did seemed eventually to solve the problem, because the engine stuttered and fired up with a puff of smoke, and to our disappointment the plane soon turned into the breeze and took off with a splendid roar. It made our day — how long, we speculated, before that would happen here again? We reckoned it in centuries — or never. What was even better was the fact that on a deserted beach we were the only ones to have seen it happen.

Sometimes when we had a bit of spare pocket money — which wasn't often — we went off to a funfair that for a year or two had appeared on the promenade past the clock tower. It was unremarkable as funfairs go except for one thing — it had dodgem boats, an attraction I've never seen anywhere else in all the funfairs I was later to take my own children to. It was different and to us, fascinating: you went round a flooded area about the size of a tennis court in what looked like ordinary dodgems, but these were fitted with higher sides, and powered by batteries; for 6d you'd get about five minutes a go — and the absolute rule was well displayed in several "No Bumping or Else" notices, a rule evident to everybody it seemed — except of course, Stanley, who "accidentally" caught me a thumping broadside that nearly sank me. While I was wondering what had hit me, he was called in by a vigilant attendant, given a rocket and sent off with the proverbial flea in his car. I waved cheerily at him as he slouched off, but he didn't respond. Temptation is such a wicked thing.

Occasionally on a Saturday afternoon Stanley and I went downtown to the cinema, a cavernous and exciting place given to cartoons and cowboy films; these expeditions needed a bit of planning though, since the price of seats usually had to be carefully budgeted for. The cheapest were front stalls at 9d, the back stalls (under the dress circle and most strategic, as well as providing cover from a variety of overhead missiles) were 1s 3d, with the dress circle at 1s 9d, and being quite out of our financial reach anyway — unless parents had been feeling generous.

Cinema visits were only partly to see the films. The main attractions were not only to keep a close eye on what was going on in the back row of the stalls where the afternoon lovers were (Stanley was pretty keen on this), but also to snipe at suitable targets with elastic band and folded paper pellets — though a pea-shooter was even better. Ideally, a suitable target would be a solitary woman wearing a large hat (an anti-social act in itself). As with everything, timing was all — so if you could tear yourself away from the pursuing sheriff's posse, guns blazing and hot on the heels of the bank robbers, that was the time to pick your target and let fly — the pellets and peas zinging and droning through the darkness. I believe that on one occasion the film had to be stopped while the manager tried to restore order, though unfortunately we missed that entertainment. Not surprisingly, ladies given to large hats were only infrequently to be found sitting in the front stalls, so it was only the stupid, or a visitor innocent enough to have ventured into the danger area who wound up as a target. You might say that Saturday afternoon cinema visits were entertaining multi-dimensional affairs well worth the financial planning required — so long as you knew the ropes and, particularly, where not to sit.

Back in the real world, girls didn't feature much in our lives, mostly we regarded them as another species to be avoided where possible but there was an exception. I think her name was Sarah and she was about our age with an annoying habit of turning up when Stanley and I were particularly busy with private and important business. The first time she arrived we were playing cricket in Stanley's garden. We fancied ourselves at cricket, bowled vicious bodyline and leg breaks at each other and broke an occasional window. Inevitably Sarah asked if she might bat. Stanley's and I looked at each other — should be easy we thought, let's humour her — a couple of bodylines and she'll go home. In our dreams. We threw everything at her and everything we threw was dispatched with exasperating ease, usually to the furthest and most overgrown reaches of the garden. We never did get her out — and we wouldn't have let her bowl either. I've never laughed at women's cricket since — nor, I reckon, has Stanley.

Those were days of freedom children couldn't be allowed today; in the holidays nobody was concerned if we were out all morning and again in the afternoon and

18

evening — and nobody seemed to worry overmuch about what we were doing either though we had to be a bit careful with our catapults — having overdone it on one occasion when we sniped at some men working on the railway line, a stupidity which caused a commotion that even Lucy couldn't cover up. That incident cost me my catapult and a three-day gating, a deprivation that bit deep — particularly as Stanley, whose parents were not advised of the incident, got off scot-free. Under normal conditions I was required to be on time for meals, which wasn't a problem as I was always hungry, and I got shoved into a bath every bedtime — Mother not wanting her Lucy-tidy house contaminated. Was I happy? In summer with Stanley, yes — totally.

CHAPTER
THREE

Shops, a Salon — and Maybe a Model

Sometimes in the holidays I would go shopping with Mother. Bexhill was a mile away and usually we would walk — but the best treat of all was to go both ways by electric trolley bus if there was going to be a lot to carry home. They were actually only single-deckers but I thought them wonderful; running pretty well silently on big rubber tyres, they were fitted with long arms stretching from roof to the overhead power lines that hissed and sparked as the arms passed along them. This limited where they could go which was only where their power lines went — and occasionally the driver would get it wrong, maybe turning so sharply that the connectors came off the wires. It was real hi-tech stuff then: he would pick up a long wooden pole carried on the roof for the purpose, and lift the sprung connectors back into place — often to a critical commentary from his passengers. For 1d you could travel for miles in a machine of itself producing no greenhouse gases or any other nasties of today — and best of all, pick-up and set-down points were at our front gate. What price progress?

Whichever way we travelled, the first stop was nearly always Sainsbury's, which was at the seaside end of Devonshire Road, the main shopping area — then we would work along by way of Longleys the drapers and Boots, which had a lending library in those days, an attraction for Mother — and finished up in the post office square with all its hoardings in front of the railway. I remember seeing that famous Guinness advertisement for the first time there: "Guinness is good for you — just think what two can do" — with a toucan pictured with a glass of Guinness balanced on its beak — an ad that still lives on today as a classic.

In Sainsbury's my job was to buy the butter, which sat in yellow mountains on the marble counter. It was weighed then shaped all ridged and glistening by the assistant's wooden paddles, to be wrapped in greaseproof paper in the required perfect block; I had to ask for "slightly salted Empire please", which came at 1s 6d a pound. Such things as rice and sugar, dried peas and beans, were dug out of sacks to be weighed rattling onto the scales with their brass weights; pre-packaging was not much in evidence then.

Bacon came in large sides at Sainsbury's, usually carried in on an assistant's shoulder to be dumped alongside the shiny red slicing machine, then carefully positioned ready to be sliced by its razor-sharp revolving blade, each rasher being caught by the assistant as it fell, to be placed neatly on the waiting greaseproof paper. It must have been a skilled job for

21

anybody — with the machine itself an accident waiting to happen — since its blade was only partly guarded and a wrong move could have cost a finger — or worse. That was the downside of the machine, but its upside allowed you to choose a range of thickness of your rashers, which is more than you can do today when you get what you're given.

Looking around the high street now, Sainsbury's, Boots, Marks & Spencer and Woolworth are about the only survivors I can remember, they were all much smaller then of course, and selling many fewer ranges of goods; in particular Woolworth sold nothing over the price of 6d which most likely accounted for its popularity in those days — everything seemed such a bargain and was worth a trawl round on pocket-money day. But it was really a time of the small shop dispensing everything you might imagine: the haberdasher for instance, with its wools, cottons and lacy knickers — but marked out as special because of the change machine. This was a small wooden container holding money from the transaction, which whizzed along a high wire across the shop to a clerk sitting in a little cubicle where he'd sort out the change, pull a lever and return it to the counter. It was a high-speed technical marvel to me.

There was also, as I've mentioned, Mr Barker's toyshop — that wonderful Mecca which so effortlessly relieved us of our pocket money. Run by a man who evidently loved toys as much as we did, it was infinite in its temptations: everything was displayed in a profusion of flying model planes, Dinky toys, games, you name it

— and it was certain to be there, even to a working model railway with its Hornby locomotives and Pullman carriages travelling endlessly through a rich countryside of village, tunnels, bridges and signal boxes — the proprietor's other world I think. He must have been a happy man, no doubt a rich one too.

It was the particular smell of those shops that keeps them sharp in my memory and I could have told you where I was blindfold — my favourite sweet shop for instance, with its dark smell of liquorice and shelves of tall glass jars of toffees, humbugs and colourful packets of sherbet. It had an overcrowded counter where two-pennyworth of bulls' eyes would be weighed out by a lady as old as time, who twirled the bag into ears to keep it shut before handing it over. There was the ironmonger's emporium with its sacks of nails which Father bought by weight, and the piles of mops and tools and shiny buckets; the paraffin-metallic scent of that pile-it-high-and-sell-it-cheap wonderland was unmistakeable, and such shops still smell the same to me even today.

Further along that street, close to the Church of St Barnabas where I was christened, was another favourite port of call — Marchant's, the bicycle paradise with its oily, rubbery atmosphere and racks of bicycles with their curvy chromium racing handlebars all just asking to be ridden. One memorable birthday, my parents took me to buy a brand new Raleigh bike with a chain case and Sturmey Archer gears, which cost the seemingly vast sum of £12 19s 6d. For that money today you might be able to buy the saddle — but I doubt it.

Least subtle of all by a long way was the fish shop in Western Road opposite the cinema (the Gaiety, if I remember right). In any weather you knew where it was long before you got there. It was open-fronted with a striped canvas awning and hung with flypapers, those long orange incredibly sticky ones that were the end of the road for dozy flies — more of a gesture on the part of the fishmonger I think, because there were plenty of very active insects everywhere else. On the white display slabs lay the dulling silvers of long-expired herring and mackerel, the rich chestnut of kippers and the dramatic red of a lobster or two, all those together with dabs, bloaters and the rock salmon Mother used to buy for our cat — each one staring at you with reproachful eyes.

Many of those on their slabs had been brought in by the local fishermen working off Bexhill beach — an enviable job I thought, with time to sit in the sun wearing a rakish cap and knubbly sweater while mending nets — with their boats laid up above the tideline, all varnished and smelling of salt and tar and goodness knows what else. I thought of early starts before it was properly light, with an old diesel engine chuntering us comfortably along, with a gaggle of gulls making a commotion far offshore — all that in perfect summer weather and a calm sea, of course — definitely a job to be considered. But I digress.

Shopping was a leisurely affair, Mother appearing to know pretty well everybody in Bexhill, so the time of day was frequently passed; this for me was the most boring and occasionally uncomfortable downside of an expedition. There was an elderly lady, elderly to me that is, who after a lengthy conversation always wanted to kiss me goodbye — the kiss of death as far as I was concerned. Each time she bore down murmuring "Dear little boy" — and poised to administer another wet one, she terrified me with her mauve lips and wattles. On one such encounter, happily the last, I must have flinched as she made her final approach — a reaction that upset her, and she flounced angrily away. Mother was not best pleased with my appalling manners as she put it, but she wasn't the target.

Poor lady, one of tens of thousands of the dispossessed, the women destined to remain spinsters long after the ravages of First World War battles such as the Somme, which on its first morning destroyed something of the order of 30,000 men before the general responsible had quite finished breakfast coffee and croissants in his behind-the-lines chateau. Her problem was her need, and not realising (or perhaps not caring) that small boys don't do tragedy, and hate being kissed.

The only expedition into Bexhill with Father was an occasional Saturday afternoon visit for a haircut at Jantzen the barber — not my favourite occupation, but one mitigated by a visit to the sweetshop for a packet of wine gums after I'd been done. The Salon (as Jantzen liked to call it) was long, large and heavy with the aromas of brilliantine and hair spray; on the back wall was a puzzling notice which enquired: "*Something for*

25

the weekend, Sir?" I never did get a straight answer about that from Father, and it remained a mystery until Stanley put me right. Six padded chairs tall enough for me to have to climb into, sat in a line in front of vast individual mirrors in which I watched myself resembling a tent with a head perched on top, being clippered and shorn to well above my ears by a white-coated barber with slicked hair and droopy moustache: short back and sides was the order — and no messing. I was then doused in a cloud of hairspray, dusted down and released reeking and cross for Father's approval. I reckon I really deserved those wine gums — though very occasionally expeditions with Father in a good mood might yield a visit to Barkers — and maybe a model aeroplane kit to go with the sweets.

I spent a lot of time in winter, and summer too when the weather kept me inside, building models — a pleasure and hobby in which I still occasionally indulge. The 1920s and '30s were a period of development and change in many respects, technology was taking off, later to be accelerated even more by war. My particular focus was on aeroplanes, an interest fostered by the fact that we had an air show with mock battles and aerobatics every year, which was flown from a big open field not far from our house; there you could get close enough to touch the planes, and for 5 shillings actually have a flight, not that I ever got one. It was all happening then, everything flying faster and faster, such as the De Havilland Comet, which made the flight to Australia in a couple of weeks or so. It seemed an amazing world to me.

My interest in modelling provided a good opportunity to work with Father who performed miracles without apparent effort and under whose instruction I slowly improved. "It would do no harm" he would often remark as he sorted out yet another of my blunders, "to read the instructions first." Eventually the wooden kits gave way to the sort of accurate plastic ones similar to those of today, and with these some reasonable models appeared on my shelves.

One in particular was the Imperial Airways passenger plane that flew over our house every day at 4p.m. on its way from Croydon to Paris; it was a dinosaur already as far as design was concerned — but still magnificent. At 2,000ft it was ear-splitting and usually on time to the minute, and sometimes I fancied I could see the faces of the dozen or so passengers looking down at me from the windows, and how I wished I could be up there with them. This was one of the first scheduled air services anywhere, starting in those early days literally from that grass field at Croydon, albeit a large one. So that particular model was the be-all and end-all of my efforts, even supplanting my Schneider Trophy Supermarine, and it came into my life as a reward for not biting my nails.

CHAPTER
FOUR

Concours and
a Cathedral

One day my aunt Elizabeth who loved cars, arrived as she sometimes did — usually without notice — but this time with a brand new Morris Oxford, a streamline state-of-the-art delight with its wonderful smell of leather and newness that cars had in those days, though an SS Jaguar with its mile-long bonnet and strap would have been even better. Without delay she entered it for fun in a Concours d'Elegance, a popular and well-publicised summer competition, which was staged on Bexhill's promenade every year. With Mother who had been cajoled into joining in the fun, and resplendent in a white slinky linen suit and large black hat — she took centre stage; showing quite a lot of silk stocking, she led the attack on the judges' sensibilities, arranged herself elegantly beside the bonnet of the gleaming car and, effortlessly it seemed, won first prize — despite the fact of there being a number of really exotic cars on display, including a Bugatti with polished exhausts and a voice that stirred my heart. It's not just the cars that win such events, I realised, a useful piece of early learning on my part. Elizabeth, full of fun and fairly fancy-free, had style: she also, I suspect, had a bit of an eye for Father — nothing provable of course. In the end she married a Canadian soldier and disappeared to Canada, and after the war I didn't, to my great regret, see her again for very many years.

Occasionally we would visit my Grandparents who lived at Herne, a small village near Herne Bay in Kent. This was a great occasion because it meant getting up very early and driving the sixty or so miles to reach them in time for breakfast. Loaded up with comics and toys of the moment, I always looked forward to that journey through changing countryside where something interesting always seemed to be about to happen. There were no motorways then and most of our journey took us through winding country roads and lanes. Once while we were driving along, Father had to avoid an enormous steaming dump of dung in the middle of the road — "elephant?" he laughed, not really believing it. A mile or so further on round a corner, we nearly rammed the contributor — doubtless feeling much relieved — an elephant bringing up the rear of a travelling circus on its way, like pilgrims, to Canterbury. What a country — with cattle chewing their cud on one side of the hedge, an elephant taking up most of the road on the other — what next? I loved those early morning drives.

Granny and Grandpa lived in a very traditional clapboard cottage, which had a large rambling garden that required fresh exploration at every visit and boasted an outdoor privy, down which you needed to put a lot of Keating's powder so you didn't have to clip a peg on your nose. The cottage was dark and beamed inside, with that unmistakeable smell that old cottages always seem to have, a mixture of polish, dust and a century or two of people living there. Over everything each time we arrived, hung the mouth-watering smell of breakfast bacon and eggs, always just about ready to put on the table, with Granny, who had one leg shorter than the other, bobbing about and fussing. Grandpa as usual, would be sitting in his chair not doing much except talking.

All our visits were the same — especially the food which I thought great: a big English breakfast, then after a visit to a hotel up the coast from Herne Bay where I was allowed a glass of non-alcoholic cider, we returned for a late lunch of cold chicken and salad with Heinz Salad Cream (which, like Marmite, tastes exactly the same today), followed by trifle. Gorged by then, I was always sent up to Granny's bed for a rest, never a problem for me when I had my comics, after which was their magic garden to explore, always the same, always different. At around 6p.m. we would get ready for the return journey, Granny would slip me half a crown (riches!) and a wet kiss — and then knackered by doing very little all day, I'd sleep most of the way home. Lovely times!

Grandpa was pretty well everything Father wasn't, the biggest difference probably being that Father was a conformist and Grandpa wasn't. Father did pretty well in the bank because he was good at saying and doing the right things at the right time; Grandpa had been in business connected with the Corn Exchange in London, and had not done particularly well for various reasons, which I never fully understood. Retirement on just about enough money suited him well it seemed; once a week in fine weather he'd make an early start (for him) and walk the twelve miles or so from the cottage to Canterbury: this I gather was more of a perambulation from one hostelry (Grandpa always called pubs "hostleries") to the next, so that by the time he reached Canterbury he was usually petty well oiled.

Well oiled or not, he would head for the Cathedral about which he had a vast and detailed knowledge, and set himself up as a very unofficial guide. He was particularly good I'm told, on the subject of Thomas à Becket's demise, the actual spot of course, and probably detailed down to the dramatic drawing of swords and spilling of copious quantities of blood, as if he'd been present at the time. After such a tour I can imagine him standing modestly at the great door with his bowler hat (he always wore a bowler like Mr Banks our builder, probably to go with his gold watch chain prominent on a tight waistcoat) — a bowler sufficiently inverted to encourage suitable donations from grateful and enlightened tourists. After all that he took the bus home, the morning's well-lubricated hike being enough for one day. He was a free spirit who was once heard to remark very late in life that, if given the chance, he'd have every minute of his time over again: not many would say that. Like my Aunt Elizabeth, he had style.

Very occasionally, probably as a matter of family solidarity, we would spend a week of summer holidays at Herne Bay with two of Father's aunts, Rose and Maud, skinny spinster ladies who ran a genteel guesthouse offering special guests like us very advantageous rates, as I often heard them put it. Herne Bay wasn't up to Bexhill's standards as far as beach and sea were concerned, it's Thames' estuary and muddy, but there were compensations in the fun fair and resident Punch and Judy show, as well as having dozens of sailing dinghies anchored just off-shore. One exciting morning after a storm, all you could see of them were the tops of their masts sticking out of a brownish innocent-looking sea.

But best of all was the fact I was usually allowed to sleep by myself in the garden summerhouse, a rickety place smelling of apples — and saved especially for privileged people like myself at even more reduced rates, as my Aunts never failed to tell me. It had a camp bed with a knobbly mattress, cobwebby rafters and a washstand with massive water jug and bowl that I never used. It was a magic place in a magic garden with loaded fruit trees asking to be climbed, a pond full of tadpoles (you don't fall into the pond, my Aunts warned severely, or else), and that tufty not-very-often-mown-grass that glistens with what look like spiders' webs in the early mornings.

Being an only child I had few problems with sleeping in the garden by myself, since it was a friendly place with its forest of trees in space enough to be prairie or jungle or anything else imagination required. But the early mornings were the garden's real speciality: I was nearly always woken at first light by birdsong — the garden and deserted streets seeming to amplify that wonderful sound: add that to air heavy with mist and the smell of sea, and you're close to perfection. Probably there were more songbirds then — certainly I've never heard anything to equal such orchestrations since those days; uncomfortable mattress notwithstanding, those moments were something I've never forgotten.

As I have suggested, travelling by road in the 1930s was often something of an adventure, not only in terms of coming across an occasional elephant. The motorcar was a much less well developed beast then, things frequently went wrong, bits dropped off, engines overheated and there was always the likelihood of a puncture. Driving the machine had its moments too, gearboxes were seldom fitted with syncro-mesh, so gear changing required skill and had to be judged precisely, with a full orchestral accompaniment if you got it wrong. Things had gone a bit further than the leather coat and goggles days, but Father was always meticulous about sorting out the car before we went any long distance: engine, jack and wheel brace were checked, a spare can of petrol, another of water — and one of those tall glass bottles of Castrol engine oil were stowed in the boot with the luggage: tyre pressures were checked, loins girded.

The business of travelling across the sleepy counties of England usually involved an AA route that took us from town to town by way of a variety of roads, main, not so main — and occasionally very not so main indeed, though Father was open-minded about the routes offered, so long as they didn't ever involve either Kingston or Exeter by-passes — he had a big thing about them. It was usually a pleasant leisurely progress if you weren't in a hurry; when you needed a fill-up, nearly every village had its own garage with a hand pump that first filled a measuring-glass container with petrol before it was pumped into your car's tank, a gallon at a time — not a very speedy process, and it would probably have been dispensing BP Ethyl at 1s 3d a gallon, a popular brand at the time.

If you had a puncture, not an infrequent happening, you changed the wheel and prayed there wouldn't be another one before finding a garage — wonderful places with their cavernous workshops and oily forecourts bright with advertisements for Castrol oils and Vimto drinks (both of which I still see around today). Such places made a good living from their puncture repairs alone — a primitive business involving a battle to extract inner tube from a bloody-minded tyre casing, before getting to the bucket of water to locate a usually elusive leak.

Some summers we went on holiday to Cornwall, a journey of about 300 miles; in the days before motorways and at speeds averaging much less than 30mph, it was more than a ten-hour drive if you did it in one go — which we didn't. That meant a night in a hotel, an aspect of travelling I loved. Usually it wasn't necessary to book ahead — when everybody got tired, we found what most likely had been a coaching inn and stopped there for the night. I remember many of those places as being old and beamed with lots of red-patterned carpets and rugs that didn't quite match, particularly those along winding passageways, which always had floorboards that creaked alarmingly underfoot. I'd usually sleep on a camp bed put up in my parents' room, which wasn't a problem as I could have slept on anything then. It was a taste of another world, since most of those inns had been accommodating travellers for centuries — they'd just swapped horses for cars, and stables for a garage often fronted by the same cobbled yard that had been there forever. The waiters wore Dickie bow ties and tails, and chambermaids who turned down the beds at night, were smart in frilly caps and aprons. The cost? Somewhere around 10 shillings, with a roast beef and apple pie dinner, plus bed and breakfast — for all of us.

It really didn't pay to be in a hurry; one afternoon somewhere in Devon, we rounded a corner to find sacks from a very large farm cart being unloaded into a granary adjoining the road. Such operations move at their own pace, and since there was no room to pass, Father switched off the engine and we waited . . . and waited. If the mindset was right, such hold ups were tolerable as well as a bit of a rest; my parents seemed relaxed enough and I was allowed to go and see what was going on. I stood watching the laboured hoisting of sacks, aware of creaking pulleys and the deep-summer smell of newly threshed grain; the farm workers were red faced, sweaty and friendly, and one of them offered me a boiled sweet from his waistcoat pocket. I sucked and watched until the cart was empty, the old tractor cranked into life, and the road cleared for traffic — of which quite a number of assorted vehicles had backed-up by then. It all took half an hour at least and I got a rocket for accepting sweets from a strange man. But it was worth it.

For all the frailties of 1930s cars, their nerve shattering back-firing, punctures and other hazards, there was a glamour about them, a panache, with their individuality of line and fitment, their big wheels with a million spokes (murder to clean) and whitewall tyres, the gleaming mascots on their radiators — all the things that made a car individual in those wonderful days before the jelly mould shape of today took over. As a small boy hooked on most things mechanical, I loved them all.

CHAPTER
FIVE

When Life Gets Real

The end of summer meant a return to the world of school, and school always loomed large, presenting its own hazards. Time lost because of peritonitis put me behind academically and I had to run to keep up; for a while life was a hassle as far as lessons were concerned, though I was lucky enough to find subjects like English and History easy to catch up on, even Latin wasn't too much of a problem. Maths though was another story, with subsequent repercussions. Collington Rise, the school I went to, was pretty much a carbon copy of at least half a dozen others in Bexhill, all distinguished largely by variations in the garish stripes and colours of blazers and caps. Plus fours were fashionable at the time among Bexhill's headmasters, they all wore them, and they all seemed to be playing golf when they weren't exhorting even greater efforts from a touchline; sport was king, with success a big factor in a school's reputation and a headmaster's income.

For my first couple of years at school, Stanley was there with me until he went off to boarding school at Sutton Valence; that was a big plus for me because we were friends enough for him not to pull rank more than necessary to keep me in my place, and he kept a bit of an eye on me as well. On one occasion he was around to sort out a situation in which a very large boy by name of Campbell, seemingly with nothing better to do, was amusing himself by straddling me on the gym floor and preparing to give me the dreaded spittle-gob treatment from a range of about 12 inches — a foul practice much enjoyed by those with a significant weight advantage. Stanley, who fortunately was passing at the time, would have none of it — and Campbell, trails of spittle and all, abruptly disappeared from that uncomfortably close focus, to reappear on the floor some yards away with Stanley heavily on top of him saying something pithy and no doubt personal in his ear. I owed Stanley a lot for that deliverance, a fact he was happy to remind me of on more than one occasion. Even today when I'm shopping in the supermarket, I recall that Campbell was almost certainly of the clan destined to profit from that well-known brand name in soups — an apposite thought as I drop a tin or two only from Heinz or Baxter into my trolley.

In the 1930s at schools like these, probably in most boys' schools of the time, much of one's learning, academic and otherwise, was apt to arrive painfully across the seat of one's trousers, corporal punishment being the norm and hardly remarked upon in days when the lash and birch rod were still used in prisons, a practice that lived on until 1960, I believe. Our headmaster whose patience burned on a short fuse, taught both English and maths; wrong spellings in an essay were corrected once and you wrote each correction out ten times. Repeat the spelling mistake in a subsequent essay and there would be a written invitation to see him in his study at some predetermined time for a caning; luckily for me my spelling was good, and I never had a dreaded "See me" at the end of an essay.

The mysteries of long division however, were quite another matter; one day I was called out to the blackboard and required by the headmaster to do a long-division sum; I stood in the dusty held-breath silence knowing full well it was far beyond my abilities, especially in a situation like that. At morning break I was called to his study.

"It seems you require a little stimulation" he remarked, thoughtfully testing a cane for weight and flexibility from a rack in his cupboard. What followed might have been called stimulation, but it did little for my long division. In the end Father patiently sorted out the problem for me, which was just as well.

Prep schools were then, and probably still are, public schools in miniature with the same characteristics of tradition in academic attitudes, religion and sport, but without the underlying military influences that I was to encounter later at Lancing. My prep school had all this plus the facilities to make them happen: there was a dedicated chapel, excellent playing fields and a swimming pool. I learned my cricket there, something taken very seriously — with an ornate pavilion and immaculate pitch and ground; white flannels and blazers were the order for big matches requiring the presence of parents — lazy tea and deckchair afternoons when mothers turned up in flowery silk dresses and imaginative hats, with fathers suffering in dark suits. To this day I still wear a split thumbnail gained by my stupidity in not wearing gloves while batting in one of those matches.

Cricket in those days enjoyed the same popularity as football does today, and all our attitudes reflected it. As I have said, my school made a big thing of it — a particular bonus of which was an annual visit to the Sussex County Cricket ground in Hove to watch an international match. A date would be established and in pristine uniform — pressed blazers, shorts, very polished shoes, we would climb aboard a green charabanc with *SOUTHDOWN* in gold twirly letters on its side, and be whisked off to Mecca at Hove. Such excitement — especially when we got to see the West Indies team who were better than anybody — even the Aussies. Were they the three W's days of Worrall, Weekes and Walcott, or did they come later?

Back in the land of reality was every-day routine. Because I lived only about a mile from school I was a dayboy — salvation no less, because it meant I got home at about 6p.m. with a bit of freedom and time enough to do my prep before bed. On dark evenings in autumn and winter, this otherwise happy arrangement had its hazards; part of my walk home involved passing a long stretch of Collington woods on the other side of the road, woods that generated the kind of rustling dark that contains all the horrors you're certain are there but can't quite see. For a quarter of a mile I would run, no, sprint the gauntlet distance, with the trees soughing

40

and creaking in the wind and my satchel banging against my back.

I hated moonlit nights most because moonlight makes for shadows . . . and shadows move . . . moonlit or dark, I broke world records on that sprint to safety, the final part of which took me with my footsteps echoing through the ill-lit perils of a railway arch with its dripping brick walls — upon one of which was inscribed Oswald Mosley's ubiquitous encircled lightning strike emblem with its runny whitewashed caption: "Mind Britain's Business", a sentiment I'd heard often enough coming from behind Father's newspaper. Did Britain ever mind its own business?

In the summer term the woods held no horrors — in fact were a good dawdling place, and the light evenings usually allowed a dash to the cliffs and sea after prep was finished — usually the best part of a school day. Later, I would lie in bed listening to Father mowing the lawn with the scent of cut grass heavy in the air; in the silence after he had finished, there came the everywhere voice of sea fidgeting with its shingle beach a few hundred yards away. For me, the highest peak of summer was the sound of the *Royal Sovereign* Lightship's foghorn booming in over twelve miles of Channel as the sky began to lighten at dawn: even on a school day that was the best start I could imagine.

Preparatory schools, the good, dreadful and indifferent, flourished in the 1920s and 1930s, especially I suspect, along the South Coast with its sea breezes and sunshine (read any brochure of the time); certainly Bexhill had its full share, and I can recall without effort, four other schools similar to mine, situated within a radius of a mile or so — the unfortunate pupils of one of them (Falconbury, if I remember right) had to wear plus fours as part of their school uniform — an ongoing source of aggravation to them. As with much else, the war put paid to many such schools, and in Bexhill as far as I'm aware, very few indeed were resurrected after 1945 with the advent of a new government, a new education act — and different social attitudes.

CHAPTER
SIX

Skating the 1930s

The 1930s were interesting times in which to grow up, a world of social extremes; Agatha Christie's Hercule Poirot playing in the films we watch today, recreate aspects of the time very well — the Art Deco days with their distinctive modernistic designs demonstrated in buildings and cars, and of course, locomotives. There was flamboyance, a freedom of colour, line and ideas, and I recall with pleasure the Clarice Cliffe breakfast set we used for years — the bright oranges and greens of the design chasing round my cereal bowl. I saw something similar auctioned in a television programme recently, it made a small fortune — I wish I'd kept ours!

The architecture of the 1930s was well demonstrated when the De La Warr Pavilion was built close to the sea front at Bexhill, in fact it featured in one of the Poirot films I've recently watched on television, and I've often glimpsed it in other programmes as well. To my eye it seemed amazing: it's a one-off, a long but not very high building of white cement with many steel-framed windows overlooking the sea, which was only yards away. Inside it had a theatre and restaurant, elegant staircases together with many other spacious areas that were used for social events and exhibitions. I saw my very first working television at an exhibition there — it had a black and white picture with a disconcerting brown spot in the middle of the screen, something they hadn't figured how to get rid of at the time. The whole building was full of light and sea-dazzle on sunny days; I think it was and still is unique, and symbolised in the very newness of its design many of the attitudes and ideas of the period. At its opening in 1936, I was one of the choir of schoolchildren (can't think why, I had absolutely no singing voice) who stood on the stage of its theatre and belted out Blake's *Jerusalem* to a frightfully important audience, many of whom had come from London for the event, not to mention my parents, together with Stanley and his parents. But as far as Stanley was concerned, it was something I was never to live down — me on a stage — singing!

What the Poirot and other films don't bring out so clearly is that brittle underlying awareness of approaching disaster, a metaphorical sword hung overhead perhaps — accelerating the frenetic gaiety rooted in the mood that had blossomed after 1918. There was much to cloud the physical pleasures of those dizzy years — but diversions were many. They were the slick days of Noel Coward, Ivor Novello and Jack Buchanan (Mother's idol); there were flighty young women in white stockings, dizzy figures hung over from the 1920s — Flappers they were called. You listened to the fashionable dance bands of Henry Hall and Jack Payne, the piano of Charlie Kunz, and picked up salacious stories of wicked goings-on in the smart roadhouses poised along the routes to practically everywhere. For those with money, the South Coast was a Mecca on the make — but the time to enjoy it was absolutely then, and not a minute later. One weekend while I was skating on the promenade, I stopped to watch the sleek outline of what I think was the Hindenburg Zeppelin flying low along the horizon, probably on its last trip to America. It looked enormous even at that distance, grey and arrogant as it cruised just outside our territorial waters, a physical reminder of trouble ahead — though if I remember right, it merited hardly a seawards glance from the sauntering passers by. Interest was focused elsewhere.

Roller skating the long mile or so of invitingly smooth tarmac of Bexhill's sea front that finished only when it reached Galley Hill, was a favourite weekend occupation for me; going like the wind with a head full of fantasies of fighter pilots shooting down German planes, I weaved in and out of strolling crowds of men in blazers and girls in floaty dresses. There were those amazing three-wheeled wicker bath chairs to be skimmed by with inches to spare, chairs containing rugged-up corpses in Panama hats, being pushed along by cheeky uniformed nurses eyeing up the swaggering Burlington Berties in their straw hats and brothel-creepers (Mother's term). There would be a military band playing old favourites to a dozing audience in deck chairs at the bandstand, hokey-pokey barrows — some with a chained monkey wearing a red or green jacket — selling vivid but risky ice cream. As the daring

45

fighter pilot I was not popular and had many a stick shaken at me as I flew in and out of the crowds, but I didn't care — I was young, silly, fit again after illness — and you don't get to feel like that very often in a lifetime.

One way and another, Bexhill before the Second World War was a swinging place with a reputation that attracted thousands. With its hotels, many of which were on the seafront, it was ripe for what the French engagingly call "Le Dirty Weekend", a particular attraction my parents were inclined to suck their teeth over (maybe it was lip service on Father's part), while Grandpa, constrained by Granny, saw nothing wrong with people enjoying themselves and bringing money into the town. Those were halcyon days for Bexhill, days ending abruptly in 1939 and subsequently taking many years to come anywhere near their former glory after 1945: perhaps it was a case of the dog having had its day.

Sport and Germany fizzed and buzzed in the radio's static every day; banner headlines alternated between test cricket drama and the latest Hitler utterance, but in a country where cricket ruled, the occasion when Len Hutton broke all records in his innings against Australia, swept aside the mundane world of politics in a plethora of triumphant headlines inches high. It was meat and drink, a diversion for millions and made Hutton the hero everybody needed, especially as it was the old enemy he had put through the mill.

To me at the age of thirteen, war seemed just an exciting prospect slotting-in with the happy diversions of cricket, fighter planes, SS Jaguar cars and expeditions with Stanley. When in 1938 the population was issued with gas masks, I was over the moon on the day I went with Mother to a crowded pavilion in our local park to be issued with ours — what excitement! The mask, smelling all rubbery, came in a cardboard box with a string attached so it could be slung over your shoulder; I carried mine home like a prize, but very annoyed because I wasn't allowed to wear the mask there and then.

CHAPTER
SEVEN

Bonfires, Barbecues and a King or Two

At a time like that I suppose it wasn't surprising there was a strong feeling of patriotism everywhere — it was "King and Country" time and obvious even to a small boy. At Christmas with Granny and Grandpa staying with us as they usually did, the King's speech was an important part of Christmas Day. At 3p.m. the radio crackling and spluttering, blasted out the National Anthem as a preliminary to the King's address: immediately Father and Grandpa sprang to their feet and stood stiffly to attention. Stuffed with turkey and pudding I followed suit, feeling it was what men had to do. Mother and Granny obviously weren't part of this ceremonial and they remained seated, though sitting up straighter and looking serious. After the speech they all relapsed into comas and I went off to play with new toys. It was what you did on a Christmas afternoon, a routine that was never varied or remarked upon.

The same spirit was abroad at the time of King George V's Silver Jubilee in 1935, which was to be a big event with all the trimmings. On the evening of the day itself, an enormous beacon was lit on the cliffs where Stanley and I carried on our various holiday activities. We had watched it grow with happy anticipation, and no doubt I exaggerate, but it was truly enormous: stacked with all the collected combustibles for miles around, it surely must have been 20ft high, with the extra incendiary encouragement of a barrel of pitch stuffed into its foundations.

Excitement ran high as we all went out for the firing, which was at a time well past my bedtime and thus another bonus; men pushed flaming torches deep into the pile — and *whoosh* — it was away, roaring and magnificent. Such fires were lit all round the South Coast that night as they had been in Armada days, and twelve miles across the bay on Beachy Head, we could see the glow of another beacon. It was like history repeating itself, with wind enough to make the great flames crackle and leap skywards with their reflections dancing on a full tide below the cliffs. That was the evening of evenings, and wonderfully late to bed.

There was more to come. The following evening an ox roast was to be the big event in Polegrove, the local football ground — and yes, if I was unusually good all day I might be allowed to go too. So satisfactorily late, we walked down to the ground and there, enormous and sweating with fat, was an ox spitted on a great iron contraption being slowly turned by a very large man wearing a stripy apron and a chef's hat. It was like a picture from a history book, except for the chef's hat maybe, the fire spluttering as the fat dripped off the great carcase into the glowing coals, with the intent fire-illuminated faces of the crowd all pushing and swaying, busy working up an appetite. I wasn't all that keen on my slice of meat when it came — it was bloody and tough, so I disposed of a mouthful in a bin when Father wasn't looking — and gave the rest to an attentive dog that evidently knew a thing or two about ox roasts.

It was an amazing evening, but for me, there was something just a touch frightening about the scene, as if we'd all been transported to another century, and I kept a firm hold on Father's hand as we pottered about — if we were going anywhere, I reckoned, we were going to do it together. There were all kinds of entertainers to go with that picture-book scene — a fire-eater, acrobats and others I don't remember, and the field flaring and sparkling with lights seemed a great fairground crammed and noisy around its Dante-like focus. It was some celebration.

In the following year the King died, a signal for more national goings-on, but all very different this time. A defunct king required national mourning long before his funeral; all radio programmes were cancelled except for news bulletins, and in between whiles the time was taken up by endless recordings of church bells and much worse, I wasn't allowed to listen to my favourite station, Radio Luxembourg. After a suitable interval there came the state funeral, the film of which I watched by courtesy of *Pathe News* at the cinema. It had a dreary magnificence overridden by black: black coffin on a black gun carriage drawn by black-plumed horses. What really intrigued me more than anything however, was the fact of the King's riding boots being placed in the stirrups of his horse facing backwards, the symbolism of which quite escaped me; had His Majesty been mounted he'd have been facing the wrong way with only his horse's tail to hang on to if things had become tricky, an engaging but not illuminating point. But the solemnity of the occasion was pretty overpowering even from a cinema screen, and in its pomp and grandeur it reflected many of the attitudes and feelings of the time.

As it happened, the King's demise wasn't an end to the excitements of the times. The Prince of Wales, for a while to be King Edward VIII — though without a coronation (which deprived me of a holiday), apparently was doing all the wrong things, being far too involved with a twice divorced Mrs Simpson — "That Woman" as she came to be known — so much so, that the couple became the main topic of conversation which included that at our dinner table, my parents being quite exercised by what was seen to be a scandal. The problem as I gleaned it, while holding my knife and fork properly and not drinking with my mouth full, was the unhappy fact that Edward was set on marrying an American, who therefore wasn't at all suitable, a reason which quite escaped me. One day I tried to clear up this baffling shortcoming with Granny who was staying with us at the time.

"Why can't our King marry Mrs Simpson?" I asked. Granny put down her glass and fixed me with her blue gaze, "Because she's an American," she replied.

"Why does that matter?" I persisted, "isn't she pretty?"

"Would you want an American for your Queen?" replied Granny with finality, and that was an end of the matter. I suspect from the bits and pieces I gathered, that this shortcoming was the one thing that really counted as far as most people were concerned, divorce and all that, as Grandpa remarked, was for the bishops. In the end of course, it all came good: Edward abdicated and was sent off to the West Indies, and his brother got the job, to be duly crowned King George VI with all the trimmings. And I had my holiday.

CHAPTER
EIGHT

Grammar, Crammer and the End of an Era

As time went on, it became painfully obvious that I wasn't going to pass a Common Entrance exam to any public school; I'd had a shot at Charterhouse and failed miserably, the headmaster in his letter of rejection doubting whether I could float even in the bottom form. So I was removed from school and handed over to a private crammer in Bexhill. It was a wonderful move. Every day I walked round to the nearby house of Willie Wells who, unsurprisingly, wore plus fours and a pince-nez. Willie was a benevolent soul who earned his crust by teaching the likes of me. With one or two other educationally challenged hopefuls, I sat every day at a green cloth-covered table in his front room to be enlightened; he took us himself for maths and English and brought in a couple of other teachers to cover the rest. At each morning break we were given a glass of milk with cream on it an inch thick and a slice of Dundee cake. At 12.30 I walked back home, had lunch and then returned for afternoon lessons until 5p.m. It was the best of school worlds, intelligent teaching, no canes and the plus of Dundee cake. How I wished my lousy academic ability had been noticed and acted upon years earlier!

It was a life that suited me ideally, though I missed the sport, and it wasn't all that surprising that in the end I did well enough to pass the dreaded entrance exam to Lancing. For me it was an unexpected academic achievement, the real significance of which — such as being a boarder and having to live away from home — hadn't really sunk in, but such success was something novel and tasted sweet. Full of myself while roller-skating along the sea front on a weekend, I'd sometimes meet a crocodile line of former school companions who were boarders and therefore stuck with such tedious boarders' activities. Those were occasions of great enjoyment. I made a point of leaning nonchalantly against the promenade railings splendidly not in uniform, and probably noisily chewing a sweet as they passed in a surly line, closely shepherded by a master who must have drawn the short straw of the day. Small boys can be very nasty, and I was certainly no exception.

At this time there were other changes in the offing. Early in 1939 Father was promoted to assistant manager at the bank and was soon to be transferred to a Barclay's branch in Eastbourne, which meant our living there and having to move from my old haunts for good. There came the hassle of selling our house, packing up and moving, all of which happened at what seemed to be horrifying speed. Suddenly there was no sea on my doorstep, no woods to hunt — and no

Stanley. That was the early summer of 1939, and there would have been changes anyway as I was due to go to Lancing in September — but it seemed a rude uprooting at the time.

Summer holidays that year arrived as usual, but weren't the same. Our new house was in a residential area, with the sea a mile away existing only as an elusive glint from my bedroom window, and there were no wild open spaces to explore. To say the least, it was definitely not catapult country. I expect I gloomed and fidgeted in a new and un-established garden overlooked by neighbouring houses — and being such a pain probably resulted in my being sent off to a Crusaders' holiday organised at a school in Seaford, next town along the coast west from Eastbourne — and from my point of view just the sort of occupation not to be stuck with in the summer holidays.

The Crusaders were a Christian organisation often to be found along the South Coast, usually to be seen conducting happy-clappy services on the beach with sand-sculpted altars and a lot of hearty singing accompanied by the metallic jingle of tambourines, all mixing with the more attractive sounds of the seaside in summer. Their holidays were held in schools rented for a few summer weeks and involved organised games and trips to historical sites, interspersed with prayer meetings. Very unfairly, I regarded those who ran the holidays as well-meaning do-gooders exuding a toe-curling bonhomie, and took myself off exploring as often as I could get away with it.

With war being so much in the air, I bought myself a pretty special sheath knife with a murderous-looking blade, a weapon that would get anybody arrested today. It represented many weeks saving of pocket money, and I wore it ostentatiously on my belt to the envy of my fellow holidaymakers. I was wearing it on the day war was declared, when my parents motored over to Seaford to collect me — that and my gas mask, I reckoned, might well come in handy later on. Father, with the diplomacy of one who had appropriate experience, advised me, out of earshot of Mother, to be careful with it and to keep it clean. That was on 3 September 1939, and on the 15 September I was on my way to Lancing with new shoes, a trunk full of uniform clothes, and no knife.

CHAPTER
NINE

Lancing, Quads and Choirs

"Buggering great place." An observation that came from Bennett while contemplating the majesty of Lancing Chapel. Bennett had farming origins and a ripeness of language that gave him a certain standing among us in those early days. He was right of course, the chapel was, and still is, a monumental pile visible for miles, aspiring to be a cathedral, someone once unkindly remarked. I saw it for the first time from the deck of one of those old coastal paddle steamers known as *Shilling Sicks* (which one day soon were destined to do their stuff at Dunkirk), while on my way from Eastbourne pier to Shanklin on the Isle of Wight for yet another Crusader holiday. I leaned on the rail of that crowded floating contraption sprayed by its thrashing paddles, and idly contemplated that distant landmark as we passed, unaware of its future significance in my life.

In most people's lives come moments of clarity, moments when a new perception moves in, and in some respect you are changed. I can think of several such moments in my life so far, all of them crucial in their way. The first of these was on the evening at the beginning of my first term at Lancing, as I stood on the steps at the bottom of the lower quad watching my parents drive away down the college hill, to vanish round the corner — then reappear, dwindling along the Shoreham road, until they crossed the toll bridge and seemed lost for ever.

What I learned, without realising the idea at the time, was that when it really comes down to it, you're on your own. It didn't hit me as clearly as that, I was bereft and frightened, with only the vaguest idea of what I had to do next, but I knew that I had to grow up — fast — and with luck might be better for it. I turned and looked at the Gothic cliffs and precipices of the school buildings with their windows reflecting a September sun — at the immaculate quad, the cloisters — and began the journey to find where I had to be. Those were, I suppose, the first steps that everybody has to take at some point — steps that carry you from childhood into the space of uncharted territory.

To us of course, everything seen through the eyes of new boys was enormous. The vaulted dining hall — a great ark of a place, seemingly containing all the boys in the world — with its high table and minstrels' gallery where the choir each Sunday sang an endless Latinate lunch grace while we salivated over the beef and roast potatoes getting cold in front of us. The world consisted of "big school", big this, big that, big everything. It was cold and draughty most of the time, with cloud swirling off the Downs like gun smoke, and blustery winds whipping in from the sea to prowl vengefully round cloister and the quads with their vivid closely mown grass — upon which only God, staff and prefects were allowed to tread.

So it was not exactly a homely place for all the Bennetts, Chatfields, Russells, Sprotts and Wells of my year, not to mention those others who have since slipped out of memory, but old Jabez Cooper our housemaster, soon due to retire, would have us think so. At the new boys' induction held in the dim cave-like confines of his study he looked us over in silence, probably with some trepidation.

"You are lucky to be in this house, which for a while is to be your home" he remarked, "it is the best and you will keep it so. If you work hard you will be happy here and do well." There was a pervasive smell of pipe smoke and antique fart in the heavily curtained atmosphere with its books and china ornaments, and from somewhere far away came the sound of a hand bell. It's strange how insignificant details like those remain stuck in memory. To me Jabez seemed incredibly ancient, stooped and small with a tonsure of hair and a lisp. He had odd eyes too, dark with a bluish rim round the pupils that fixed on you with a peculiar intensity; it wasn't easy to lie to Jabez as we learned, nor was it advisable.

That was September 1939 with the war a few weeks old, but there were other conflicts a lot closer to us than that. New boys were at the bottom of a very large pile and it didn't take long for us to be made aware of it. What we learned to do pretty soon was to keep eyes down and mouth shut. You fagged for house captains and prefects who shouted most of the time: we made their tea and cleaned anything they put in our way, which was a lot and often. In between everything else we slept in a chilly dormitory with its polished floors and high windows. Red and black striped blankets on the beds provided colour to offset the grey stone of walls that echoed to the hand bell that turned us unwillingly out of bed every morning.

What we did each at our own pace was to grow a metaphorical shell, a kind of first line of defence. The practical place to do that was in bed — operational from lights out at 9p.m. with no talking; it was your retreat and the only place you could feel alone. You could come to grips, or not, with the day you'd just lived in: Latin, French irregulars, food, football and house captains' teas being the usual mix — a mix that grabbed you differently on different nights depending on what the day had left with you. Sometimes I'd put my mind to figuring out what I'd done to be sent away from the familiar world of home and Willie Wells, to this cold busy place where you were the size of an ant. Something pretty bad I figured, though my parents never said anything. Must have been that window I broke when I was batting for England and whacked the ball through the covers for four — it skidded off the garden wall and did for the bathroom window, but by the time I'd drifted that far I was usually asleep.

We all did variations of that, when everybody's in the same boat you get to know how the others ticked. The great thing about being young in those days was a near unconscious ability to accept without question everything about the situation we found ourselves in. It wasn't just the fact and threat of sanctions that kept you in line, more than that it was an unquestioning acceptance of the day-to-day status quo. There was one implicit irony that I didn't latch on to for years. Smoking was a serious offence and if you were caught at it you'd be caned. That was an inflexible rule set up and enforced by a headmaster who chain-smoked. It was not an absurdity to us, just a fact of life, a small part of a well-oiled system in place to produce the sort of disciplined conformity seen to be what tradition and the nation required.

Getting the hang of all that was a prerequisite for a reasonable next five years; if you slotted into the regime and were passably good at sport, which took precedence over most things, you'd be most likely to wind up in a comfortable senior position a few years later. It was as simple as that but it took me a while to do the slotting-in bit, which was nothing more than a hands-on course in the essential skill of learning how to adapt to what often seemed an extraordinary world.

There was a strong military flavour underlying our lives at school in those days of 1939, one that had been around for many years since before the First World War no doubt, and gaining strength as war clouds gathered over Europe throughout the 1930s. There was a full-blown armoury under the dining hall, heavy with the scent of gun oil used on the Lee Enfield rifles racked neatly round the fat pillars that held the dining hall up. For me, it was a remarkable and exciting place, full of memorabilia and dramatic pictures of dire moments in battle with bemedalled figures striking heroic attitudes. I was particularly impressed by one piece of memorabilia — a windscreen taken from a First World War Sopwith Camel fighter plane, which had stopped a bullet in combat: the thick glass was heavily starred by the impact, but had saved the life of the pilot who had been an old boy of the school. It was great stuff for a fourteen-year-old!

A resident regular Army RSM and his junior, a CSM, both complete in First World War uniforms and fierce waxed moustaches, were on permanent posting to the school during those early war months, and Thursday in particular was their day. There was no sport and no options on a Thursday afternoon, it was officers' training corps time; we were issued with scratchy First World War uniforms: flat caps, button-to-the-neck tunics that sandpapered your skin, breeches, puttees and brown boots. Those puttees! Invented in India probably as protection against snakes, you wound them from boot to knee — that was the idea anyway. Impossible bloody things — you either wound them so tight that your legs felt as though they were going to drop off, or so loose they unwrapped as you marched, to be gleefully trodden on by those behind you.

On those Thursday afternoons we marched with sloped or otherwise perched rifles heavy on our shoulders behind the band; to and fro across the gravelled parade area below the lower quad we tramped to the thump and squawk of drums and bugles, while majestic ahead of all was the CSM leading Mardi the

OTC goat. Mardi, beard, balls and all, was as bloody minded as his master and made a special point of leaving behind him a well-distributed line of droppings for us to tread in. Overseeing, and more or less controlling the whole spectacle from the steps of the lower quad, stood the ramrod figure of the RSM, swagger stick under arm, boots polished to a dazzling glitter; he was seldom satisfied with our clumsy efforts and his voice would effortlessly rise several octaves as his frustration increased.

At other times we did weapon training and pored over maps, field-craft manuals, and all the other things judged to be appropriate to our characters — as well as the needs of a war machine that was slowly creaking into action. I even had a few lessons learning to play the bugle, but progressed little further than producing what approximated to a series of strangled farts, and was soon told to go away. In fact this stuff (not the bugling) came in pretty handy to those of us who later joined the army and found ourselves at some basic-training unit like Maryhill Barracks in Glasgow, which later was destined to swallow me up for a while. There we found ourselves to be miles ahead of recruits who hadn't been away from home and received the training we'd cut our teeth on for years. Fitter, better disciplined, we found life a lot easier in those horrid six weeks everybody had to endure while the army bashed some semblance of a soldier into us. I've often heard it said that public-school life fits you admirably either for prison or the army: the originator of that thought had a point. But I'm ahead of myself again.

So Thursday afternoons came and went, and even Mardi and his masters had their good sides though we didn't appreciate them at the time. What was quietly much enjoyed by most of us was Field Day, an occasion which happened once a year during the summer term. It was meant to be an exercise to put into practice what we were judged to have learned of military matters during the year. Complete with rations stowed in our knapsacks and a clip of five precious rounds of blank ammunition, we were marched a very long way to somewhere like Chanctonbury Ring high up on the Downs, getting well plastered with slippery chalk mud if it had been raining.

You either attacked or defended the ring or wherever else it happened to be — either way it was a shambles. The important part was the issue of those blank cartridges — you could do all sorts of things with them, the most popular was to slide a pencil down the barrel of your loaded rifle, look for a suitable target and fire. A blank cartridge-projected pencil goes very well and is pretty accurate up to about 20yds. On one occasion a popular target happened to be a boy who rejoiced in the name of Bean (perhaps an ancestor of today's Mr Bean?), who received several high-velocity pencils in his backside. There was a lot of shouting about that, particularly from Bean, who was supposed to be fighting for us. Fortunately a lot of rifles were being fired at the time so nobody was identified as an assassin and it all blew over — well, maybe not for poor Bean.

Nobody would actually voice the thought, but field day was much enjoyed as time away from the routine of conjugating Latin verbs and the like. On a fine day the Downs were a good place to be, you could see for miles and there were skylarks everywhere, unfazed even after the racket of what passed for battle. It was good to relax on the grass after victory or defeat and work your way through the gut-filling stodge of field day rations, comfortably watching cloud shadows chasing across contour and valley. It was time out, something different and therefore welcome, and even the prospect of a long march back with the grind of getting dried chalk off boots, puttees and practically everything else, didn't spoil the moment.

The Downs played another part in our lives. Cross-country running was a big thing in the sporting calendar, not really surprising given the nature of the country around Lancing. If you were under sixteen you ran a three-mile course and those over sixteen did five miles, both of which were demanding, the Downs' contours being what they are; in particular, the five-mile course finished at the end of a marshy stretch, which had half a dozen well-filled dykes between you and the finishing line, each one just too wide to jump. There were school and inter-house events in winter, all taken very seriously with colours to be won and Brownie points to be stored up for the future — and everybody had to run regardless of whether it was purgatory or pleasure. Being tall and skinny, I found distance running not to be a problem and the Downs are lovely to run on, the turf being short and springy; a great advantage as far as I was concerned, was the fact that it involved something you did more or less by yourself, a bit of a bonus in a very communal life. Anyway, once I'd developed the legs for it and sorted out my breathing, it was something I enjoyed and did well enough to keep me out of trouble.

CHAPTER
TEN

The Loving Cup and a
Concert That Wasn't

As I said, it was a communal life in which you lived by houses and the only time you met people from other houses was in chapel twice a day, during lessons and at mealtimes although even then it was from a distance, as you ate at separate tables. I suppose this was basic to college philosophy: keeping the six houses separate tended to foster a competitive spirit and improve, perhaps, individual performance in the all-important sport. What it didn't do was to encourage inter-house friendships — in fact generally we knew little about life outside our own particular kingdom, which while not making for actual hostility, did little for any warmth on the few occasions we found ourselves together. On track or playing field they were the enemy, and while things changed in the much more relaxed days of our Moor Park era still to come, this fostered house feeling was usually a telling factor in our lives.

After morning classes, sport or whatever it happened to be, took up the afternoons except for Thursdays of course. Evening school you did in your houseroom sitting on well-polished benches at even more well-worn and scarred tables; there were two sessions of this, broken by half an hour for supper: that was the time of cocoa and "the college bun" — enormous wooden trays of buns with shiny brown tops and a maximum of one currant in each bun. The half-hour of supper was like half time at a match with everybody starving for it — and with blood-sugar level restored by your notional currant, second evening school seemed more relaxed with an achievable prospect of a few minutes' free time before bed. House captains supervised evening school to ensure that it was a scratching pen on paper kind of quiet that prevailed, a quiet you didn't mess with by whispering. Actually, it was precious time when you tried to make sense of what you thought you had learned at morning school, a time of essay and insoluble maths, so nobody pushed his luck.

On the last evening before we broke up for Christmas that year, a loving cup of some dark dubious wine was passed round the assembly in a large silver cup — a house trophy. When it came to your turn you intoned "*Floreat Nostra Domus*" in a loud voice, then you took a sip and passed it on. Actually the wine smelled quite nice, a bit like the cooking sherry Lucy kept in the kitchen for trifles, but when my turn came, I was suddenly aware of a large dollop of what looked suspiciously like spit floating on top of it: evidently somebody was expressing non-conformist feelings. I took a pretended sip and passed it on; I reckon there must have been as much wine left at the end of the round as there had been at the start, but fortunately despite the awful fury displayed by high authority when the addition was noticed, the spittle's originator was never identified. Our loving cup ritual was never quite the same after that, for me anyway.

Being of the Woodard Foundation, religion was a big thing with Bennett's Chapel to add dignity and draughts to the proceedings. We attended chapel morning and evening, while on Sundays there were also house prayers taken by Jabez at 9p.m. before bedtime. This was marked by the fags, known as "underschools", "cleaning" the houseroom before prayers began — an effort marked only by the amazing amount of dust thickening the air. When Jabez arrived you could just about make him out as a ghostly figure through the fog. The odd thing was that this apparently was never noticed or acted upon: on Sunday evenings — dust ruled OK. Tradition? I never asked.

As far as religion was concerned, I never got on with the Woodard idea. It was symbolic perhaps that one of the first things I did at Lancing was to flood the chapel. My allotted place was beside a radiator and I must have fiddled with something vital during our devotions. The first I heard of trouble was a summons after breakfast from the headmaster who evidently hadn't taken long to work out who the culprit was: such a summons was bad news as I'd learned at prep school. Quaking, I presented myself to the presence who boomed and roared a lot but who, to my considerable relief, sent me off to the armoury for a bucket and mop with instructions to clear up the mess and not repeat the offence — or else. Supervised by the CSM who didn't trust boys with buckets or anything else for that matter, I swabbed and mopped until the considerable area was slightly less wet than before. That made me late for lessons and matters weren't improved by the Latin master's response to my reasons for being late as he thought I was being insolent.

You had the full Monty as far as chapel was concerned, partly because the chaplain fancied his voice, and much of a service was intoned with the acoustics helping out. But ritual and dressing-up, the grand sense of solemnity, were unexpectedly disturbed on one famous occasion by an unfortunate boy absent-mindedly pulling a table-tennis ball from a pocket with his handkerchief. Released from captivity, it pinged and bounced its happy way down the long length of aisle — this at a point in the service when silence was absolute. Several hundred eyes followed its jolly progress with avid interest, and when it finally came to rest, an audible sigh rose from an unusually attentive congregation. There was no obvious response from authority — I believe that came later.

By comparison with what I've heard about other schools at that time, Lancing was pretty civilised in many ways. The famous alliterative three B's of public schools: beatings, buggery and bullying did not, as far as I was aware, obtain to any significant extent. Head of house prefects could and did beat, but only with the sanction of a housemaster or in more serious cases, of the headmaster. In my house such painful events were more the exception than the rule. Certainly too, there

70

were occasional relationships between older and younger boys (pretty little boys were called Twinks) but I think these were more of the "crush" variety than anything of greater significance, and as senior and junior boys slept in separate dormitories, there was little opportunity for clandestine meetings at night and with few chances by day either.

A house hierarchy was something accepted as a fact of life: attitudes and behaviour reflected where you were in the pecking order, and within its context it worked pretty well; inevitably though, there had to be somebody who was particularly disliked and who upset the pattern of things. In my first year we had a house prefect, an individual who was very much in this category; for his sins he fancied himself as a musician, in particular as a conductor. So nobody was amazed when we learned we had, as a house, been entered for the college choral competition — such was a prefect's authority: this naturally involved a lot of practice at inconvenient times (our free time), and went on far too often for enthusiasm to survive for long.

Eventually the evening of the competition arrived, houses were assembled and much choral work was performed. Wagner was our prefect's choice, a piece from *Tannenhauser* but on the night it was a lemon from the start: "*once more with joy my home I shall see*" creaked and stuttered, our unhappy conductor and his wand gesticulating frantically to get us together. I being totally junior never heard whether the inevitable disaster was due to conspiracy, or whether it was just a case of incompetents being asked to do too much by

71

another incompetent. At any rate, as a choir we slithered and slid into an uneasy silence long before poor *Tannenhauser* got anywhere near home — this to generous applause from the other houses, largely because they were enjoying our humiliation so much. And that was that. Needless to say, I don't recall there ever being any other choral competitions in my time at Lancing and perhaps it was a lesson learned by all would-be conductors with aspirations.

The sanatorium situated on the draughty edge of the Downs above the rest of the college itself, was regarded as a place of pilgrimage and sanctuary, having a sort of Blighty image as seen from the trenches. You worked hard to get there and stayed as long as possible, thus removing yourself from the rigours of daily life. You could also, if things went well, be in a position to enjoy the spectacle of your less fortunate friends sweating off on a house or school run towards Lancing Ring, that group of trees on top of a ridge of Downs, often a long wet distance away. I managed a visit to the sanatorium only in my first term when I contracted German measles; it was entirely satisfactory but lasted nowhere near long enough. I lay in a bed much more comfortable than mine in the dormitory, not feeling particularly ill, while consuming large quantities of lemonade. My companions, similarly afflicted, were able to enjoy the many benefits available as much as I — and all things considered, we had an companionable time that was only spoiled when we were unexpectedly kicked out far too soon, we thought, into the real world. It didn't take long to settle in to that gentler regime, one almost with home comforts — and to our skiving souls it was much more than just a case of being any port in a storm.

CHAPTER
ELEVEN

Without Labels

That long summer term of 1940 was following its course of cricket and the looming prospect of exams, when we were assembled one memorable morning, to be informed by a gloomy headmaster that the college was to be evacuated — ultimately to Ludlow in Shropshire, though the remainder of term would be spent either at Ellesmere or Denstone (other Woodard schools) depending on which house you were in. Apparently being close to the sea might have made us vulnerable in the event of a German invasion, but it was hinted that the real reason for our evacuation was the Navy. Needing a new land-based establishment, it had its eye on the place — and in those days what the Navy wanted — it had. At any rate, we were to pack our bags and take the train to pastures new which was an exciting prospect nicely removed from the usual routine of verbs and stuffy classrooms.

At a time in the war when things were pretty much as bad as they could get, everything seemed remarkably normal as we trundled our way through a dozing south of England. We eventually parted company with our old Southdown charabanc at a grubby Paddington Station already without some of its glass because of Luftwaffe attention. Standing with our cases on the platform, it was a moment of truth for me as the familiar green shape of our bus disappeared — it was going home, and I wasn't. After that nothing seemed to be quite the same. But doubts about our future were soon pushed aside at the arrival of our train. The Great Western Railway was taking us on our way, and the arrival of the great snorting beast of an engine had its usual fascination. Engines then had a glamour that has long since passed, and *Sir Galahad* (if I remember correctly) in all his polished and reeking glory disappointed nobody.

Train journeys at that time tended to be lengthy and unpredictable because of bombed tracks and scrambled timetables that apparently had little bearing on reality, and for hours we sat in a dusty crowded compartment watching another world unfold as we headed by fits and starts northwards and west. I was seeing a different landscape from the open rolling Downs of Sussex: now the country was taken up by sharper hills and forest, a harder land, but still with its fields lazy with cattle in the sun. Now and again we'd pass an embankment blackened and still smouldering from the sparks of other passing engines, bringing in its scent of musky sweetness through our open window. To me it was a familiar touch of home in a foreign world.

We clattered through black towns with factories and smoking chimneys, and at the stations where we stopped the platforms, often without glass in their roofs, were busy with army squaddies loaded with packs and kitbags — like us, on their way to unknown destinations. I can't remember the route we followed, but focused by the soldiers, piles of broken glass — and once a raw crater in a field beside the track, it showed us the first realities of a war that up to then had been a distant but rather exciting subject of speculation.

But even the longest journey has to end and we eventually found ourselves at our destination where to our horror, no bus waited for us.

"This is where we get a bit of exercise", instructed one of our accompanying masters, "it's where we get into line two abreast and follow me. Ellesmere School is only about a mile, and we'll all make our way there with happy smiles and no trouble. Won't we?"

So, two by two but without the happy smiles, we entered the ark of our host school. Although we were without labels round our necks, we were soon made to feel the indignity of being evacuees, by the overtly hostile inhabitants of this foreign school with its strange tribal customs and strictly enforced "Keep Left" system round its polished parquet corridors.

"Ah, the five thousand" remarked a voice louder than the rest as we trooped sheepishly into the dining hall for breakfast next morning — "and we've got to feed them, really!" To be fair, I expect our attitude to foreign legions would have been just the same if the situation had been reversed as schools really are tribal places.

Food soon became an issue. Up to then I think we'd been fortunate, but pretty soon the inevitability of rationing kicked in; there wasn't much on our plates any more, and it didn't take us long to learn to fill up on a mustard sandwich and a mug of weak sugarless tea. Well, we had to learn sometime. Our quarters were in a large draughty gymnasium with a leaky roof, situated on the far side of a large playing field; we had each been given a couple of blankets and a straw mattress and not much space on the bare boards between neighbours. However I counted myself lucky, as on one wet night, I discovered that I wasn't under one of the many leaks.

We had our classes in an imaginative variety of locations — one of which happened to be a cricket pavilion redolent with the rich aroma of generations of sweaty socks and linseed oil; how much we learned from lessons often delivered by distracted staff is open to question, and I don't think anybody worried much about that — what really mattered was the glorious fact that there were no end of year exams to be suffered. Improvise and adapt was the name of the game, and we soon settled into what in many ways was almost a holiday in a pretty good spell of weather.

All things considered, what must have been an administrative nightmare for the staff; was managed brilliantly, and the cauldron of two disparate schools seethed and bubbled but never boiled over. In fact, though nobody would admit it, we almost got to like each other, even to the extent of playing a cricket match without starting a third world war. For us it was a new experience involving a taste of harder living than we were used to, and one way and another, it did us all a lot of good by giving us an idea of a very real world to come.

CHAPTER
TWELVE

Shotguns, Pitchforks and Minnows in the Sky

Those 1940 summer holidays at the end of my first year at Lancing were spent in my Aunt's cottage at Prestwood, a village near Great Missenden in Buckinghamshire. My parents thought Eastbourne to be too dangerous for school holidays at that time, so Mother travelled up to be with me, leaving Father to fend for himself at home. In the early days of the war, Eastbourne had been reckoned safe with many London evacuees being sent there, much to the horror and amazement of local residents who had no clue of how children from the London slums looked or lived. But pretty soon the place was deemed too dangerous for evacuees, something of an irony because most of them had gone home in time for the Blitz anyway — not able to stand the place or people. But dangerous or not, I didn't get home those holidays.

Not that it mattered. We stayed in an old thatched cottage recently bought by my Aunt Elizabeth who was living there. It was heavily beamed and its thatch reached almost to the ground on the garden side. Best of all, it was permeated by the timeless smell of its paraffin cooker, a smell that still instantly conjures up memories of a summer that included my bicycle, a borrowed air rifle and Stanley, whose parents hadn't taken much persuasion to let him loose for the holidays with me. The perfect weather that was to be a backcloth to which the Battle of Britain was set and stayed set fair. Of all holidays those weeks were the most idyllic for me, though not so good for Mother who must have worried about leaving Father at home, though in fact things didn't hot up in Eastbourne until later in the war.

I remember Buckinghamshire as being beautiful with its beech woods and the quiet tucked-away villages of those times long before commuters and green wellies arrived from suburbia, and Stanley and I cycled endlessly on roads that petrol rationing had made nearly deserted. We went to a very civilised cinema in Amersham where it was safe to sit in the front stalls (we worried about this on our first visit), and enjoyed Bob Hope, Bing Crosby and Dorothy Lamour doing their *Road To . . .* films. I can't remember where all those roads led to, but I think Zanzibar was one, and suitably exotic. We fought incredibly brave battles with our air rifle against invading Germans and marauding local boys in the deep-shadowed beech woods, we didn't wash much and ate everything in sight. Mother and Aunt watched us with trepidation as the food disappeared, but somehow continued to do a brilliant job, probably going without themselves.

As a kind of background to our other activities, the Battle of Britain preliminaries were in progress and sometimes we'd glimpse a flash of silver minnows teasing a blue infinity of sky, and hear the faint drone and scream of stressed engines. Once when we were having a picnic in a large exposed field (my Aunt's choice), she became extremely uptight about our red thermos flask which she thought might attract attention — and was even more put out when we fell about laughing. Stanley and I watched those minnows diving and spiralling in that cloudless sky — every one seemed a Spitfire or Hurricane on the tail of a Messerschmitt. To us the war was a wonderful adventure we were missing and we grumbled endlessly at being too young to go and fight. Such was the background of that amazing summer, week after week of sun and brooding heat that made the narrow shady lanes cool and inviting. We were always on the move, busy with something interesting for pretty well all the daylight hours; at night we slept like the dead and as far as I was concerned, life had never been so good.

Later, the days carried a sharper and more personal edge — apart from the air battles. It was a time when the possibility of a German invasion had become a real threat. In that event we heard that all church bells were to be rung as a signal the invasion had started, a decision not popular with the campanologists of the time, since they were barred for years from ringing their bells — probably the first time since church bells were invented. We were further reminded that war wasn't just a matter of newspaper headlines, when a couple of bombs and some incendiaries were dropped near the village one night, fortunately not killing anybody but doing for a house; of course we couldn't wait to get to the site, and were rewarded by finding the tail fin of an incendiary still satisfactorily warm though somewhat bent — but still a great prize.

On our bikes we were soon reminded of invasion's possibility by the fact that most signposts had been removed by order of some genius at the War Office, who had doubtless assumed that any invaders would have forgotten their maps. Signposts that had not been removed were turned so they pointed in the wrong directions, an additional touch of insight that gave Stanley and me problems sometimes. We would get to a crossroad or T-junction, sit down on a bank and argue; once tetchily engrossed without any clue about which way to go, we saw what must have been the first of the Home Guard marching down the lane towards us — and yes, they were in shirtsleeves carrying shotguns and pitchforks sloped or otherwise perched on their shoulders. Not yet uniformed, except for their sergeant, whose tunic with its incredibly white stripes didn't quite match his trousers, they were making do with armbands marked: LDV (Local Defence Volunteers) — *Dad's Army* in embryo.

Not seeming to be in much of a hurry, they were halted without any great precision and the sergeant came over to where we sprawled by our bikes. We told him we were lost because the signposts had been removed.

"Should be in the army" he remarked with a very serious face, "big lads like you messing about on bicycles and getting lost — unless of course, you're spies — are you spies?" It would have been fun to say yes — I thought about it briefly, but didn't dare. After more pleasantries he pointed us in the right direction and then with a wave, he got his troops going again, probably off to their local pub. Stanley and I watched them out of sight and sighed, the irony was not lost on us that we probably knew more about military matters than they did — at least at our respective schools we'd fired blank cartridges in anger — or at least with evil intent. That made us feel a bit better, and we found our way home without further argument.

That summer of 1940 was a holiday never to be repeated, marking the end of one era and the beginning of another, and not just for us, since up to then — apart from the air battles — it had been a slack water time for months, but suddenly the war got going in earnest in France. Stanley and I went our separate ways at the end of those holidays, seldom to see each other again. After he left I was bereft, for he had been something like a brother to me — now suddenly a companionship of many years had apparently come to an end, but with a different finality: even though he had gone to boarding school a couple of years before me, we had lived only a few hundred yards apart, and in the holidays we found that contiguity soon filled gaps after being apart for a term. But from then on we were to be towns apart at a time when transport was a very different proposition from the days of peacetime and the so-called Phoney War of 1939 and early 1940. In fact we met only a handful of times after that, our lives developing in opposite directions — except for one memorable occasion when we met, against all the odds, somewhere in Holland, I think, early in 1945.

CHAPTER
THIRTEEN

By God, Gaslight and the Groves

I think of those years when Lancing was evacuated to Moor Park near Ludlow in Shropshire, as the *Casablanca* days — from the Bergman and Bogart film with its haunting songs that caught so well the on-the-edge mood of that time: it was a seminal film, opening my adolescent eyes to an adult world where love and loss were writ large in a period when for us, the war was going very badly indeed. How music speeds memory! I've only to hear those songs to be back through a lifetime in a flash. It was a period when I first tasted freedom under a somewhat bewildered ad hoc school regime that by the very nature of the situation had to relax most of the strictures that had bounded our lives at Lancing. It was a case of the proverbial ill wind, for in that safe backwater somewhere midway between Shrewsbury and Hereford; I spent a very different three years that I still look back on with pleasure today.

It was another world and in truth there was little that wasn't different, and for me it was a renaissance. The six school houses were distributed among a number of large not-quite manor houses in the area, places that most likely had been built around the late nineteenth and beginning of the twentieth centuries by men who had made their pile in industry and wanted status and a country retreat. In most cases it was just one of the school houses that was billeted at each of the would-be stately homes — but my house, Olds, together with Gibbs house, were allocated to Moor Park, which happened to be the largest of all our new homes.

Moor Park, which is situated about three miles from Ludlow was, and still is, an attractive rambling red-brick building set in extensive grounds that included a tennis court and lake, the whole property being bordered by woods and fields. Because of its size a considerable number of us fitted in pretty well, although the staff had to find accommodation elsewhere, except for the housemasters who lived in. With the headmaster and his wife occupying the more salubrious parts of the building — the polished floor and panelled areas — they remained somewhat separated from the rest of us, except at meals when we all ate together; the headmaster and family, staff and the two prefects sat at a separate table placed at the head of the rather elegant well-proportioned dining room, with the proletariat safely below the salt.

In 1940 such luxuries as electricity hadn't yet got as far as remote places like Moor Park, the technology of the time using gas piped in from the gasometers in Ludlow. This system provided our light, the igniting of which was often a tricky matter of spent matches and burnt fingers. Light was produced by gas mantles, cobwebby delicate things lit by a match while turning on the gas. This illuminated the mantle with a hiss, producing a hard brilliant light that served its purpose well. Gas lighting like everything else was accepted without question — though I suspect it must have been a niggling worry for the staff. In civilised circumstances, which schools certainly are not, gas lighting would probably present few difficulties. But problems arise as soon as somebody discovers that a gas mantle will disintegrate into red-hot bits and pieces of cobweb and clay when struck by a well aimed paper pellet propelled by an elastic band. Such vandalism became a serious disciplinary matter, but during my time it was frequently irresistible enough to invite target practice — particularly if some unsuspecting victim was sitting underneath the target light.

As I recall it, there was no heating at Moor Park apart from occasional open fireplaces in some of the rooms — certainly there was no provision for any radiators, or indeed much hot water, though there had to be a boiler somewhere which reluctantly provided tepid water for a weekly bath. It may have been the fact that we were, so to speak, living in the "below stairs" part of the house, and such comforts were to be found only in the headmaster's quarters.

In our houseroom there was provision for an open fire, which in winter was kept well stoked up with fuel brought in from the woods around us, a job nobody minded doing since, in theory, there was something in it for everyone. The inevitable problem in a community where pecking order ruled was that with only a single fireplace, half a dozen seniors would always sit on the brass fender in front of it hogging the heat and keeping the rest of the room cold — a situation that didn't go down well with those who were remaindered. Eventually, some bloody-minded member of the chilly majority fed up with being excluded, took it upon himself to register general disapproval. Somehow undetected, he smuggled a firework into the newspaper and kindling wood, which was always set-up ready for the next fire to be lit; on a cold winter afternoon at fire-lighting time with the seniors comfortably ensconced, the inevitable happened. The explosion was well judged (just think what a thunderflash would have done!) being small, but large enough to dislodge enough soot and debris to cover the incumbents of the hearth in a satisfactory manner without significant damage — except to dignity. The culprit was duly identified, flogged and martyred, but the happy outcome was that fire hogging by anybody, senior or otherwise, was forbidden henceforth by the housemaster, and we were all the warmer for it.

There were advantages and disadvantages to being based at Moor Park. We were, so to speak, at regimental headquarters and therefore under the eye of the headmaster and his family who, though somewhat removed, seemed always near enough to spot the untoward. But the advantage that outweighed everything was that most lessons, except for physics and chemistry, were conducted at or around Moor Park itself, which meant we were on base and didn't have the long cycle ride that the poor souls from other houses had to suffer to reach us every morning. That counted for a lot. Shropshire, with Wales at its elbow can be particularly wet at times; Heads house, I can comfortably report, had something like a ten-mile round trip every day, Monday to Saturday.

Fundamental to this wonderful difference was the fact that it was essential for us to have our bicycles, which meant that authority could no longer restrict us to specified bounds — except pubs. We did our science in the labs of Ludlow's Grammar School, and played most of our football and cricket on the playing fields at the far side of town, which put them more than three miles distant, so bikes were crucial, cherished and messed around with like cars are today. I was into gears at the time since hills were an issue, and fitted a complicated Derailleur assembly to my existing three-speed Sturmey-Archer gears: this in theory gave me nine speeds and mostly it did — but it had an irritating habit of discarding the chain at inopportune moments. So, very reluctantly, I went back to the boring three speeds, and sold the assembly to somebody in Heads house who was stuck with the ten-mile daily stint, and wasn't aware of its little foibles.

In essence, daily life at Moor Park followed the same pattern of activities as it had at Lancing in Sussex: lessons still took up the mornings, and sport the afternoons, except on Thursdays when the OTC still ruled. As far as this was concerned, since we were without the expertise and vocal additions of the RSM and CSM, who had presumably returned to other more arduous army duties, we were spared the parading and ear-splitting efforts of the band — much to our relief. We spent the time on matters like compass and map-reading with occasional mini exercises in and around the Moor Park grounds, which if not exactly battle-winning affairs, at least were fun and occasionally involved blank ammunition. Later on, duties with the Home Guard for those of us who were old enough to enlist became a new and rather more interesting addition to our military education.

A year into a school career and you're more or less settled into the life, know what's what, and are in a position to look down on the next crop of new boys. Adapt or suffer was the name of the game — and most of us adapted pretty well. Cold impersonal dormitories had given way to a range of bedrooms accommodating anything up to half-a-dozen inmates, and straightaway we recognised this as a big plus, being a lot more homely and comfortable than the endless expanses of where we'd slept before. Any adapting to be done had to do with the fact that there was only one lavatory at our end of the house for night use: perched on a dais and resplendent with its vast mahogany seat, it was of distinctly cantankerous disposition — and in any case was inevitably occupied at desperate moments.

The lavatories at Lancing were known as The Groves (always expressed with the definite article): this rather gracious term seemed to suggest the comfortable image of a gentleman's retreat; so something like: "just off to the Groves, old boy — care to join me?" was a conceit that appealed to me, and certainly in their way they were quite palatial. However, those provided at Moor Park had suffered a serious downturn in prestige and quality. A line of chemical closets had been installed about 50yds or so from the house itself: these were divided into not very private compartments by means of hessian cloth stretched over wooden frames, all under a rain-echoing corrugated-iron roof. Thus accommodated, we would sit in a companionable line and pass the time of day, often with a queue outside in the wet exhorting the incumbents to get a bloody move on.

As I suggested, flexibility is an asset especially at school, so The Groves at a distance by day presented few problems. At night, however, with an inside lavatory usually occupied or out of order, moments of desperation were a different matter. Deep country at night is dark, and nowhere is darker, more populated by owls, Dracula and things that snap twigs at your elbow, than Shropshire at 2a.m. during that 50yd dash to salvation. A dense wood cracking its knuckles on one side of the track, a high brick wall guarding an orchard and vegetable garden on the other, left but one option — speed — and a firm resolution to steer clear of prunes in future.

CHAPTER
FOURTEEN

Masters, Saints and Brass Monkey Places

I still didn't find the academic side of life easy — getting through Common Entrance didn't mean I was any great shakes at academe, so I had to plough on, get my head down and work for my School Certificate which loomed large in the not-so-distant future. Looking back, it seems to me that there were those among the staff who weren't up to much as teachers; younger members had been sucked into the melting pot of war, leaving the unfit and those who appeared to be more than somewhat past it, to guide our young lives. There was a time-honoured idea that if you'd been to university and obtained a degree of sorts, you could therefore teach, an absurdity prevalent even today. With years of hindsight, I still feel that many of the masters with whom we struggled would have been a lot happier doing something else; I'm trying to be fair — we weren't for the most part particularly bright, so they weren't on a good wicket either. But when I eventually began teaching, the first method I adopted was to remember how things had been approached in my classroom days, then to work out something completely different. I found it to be a good starting point.

It had become evident that several of the staff had worked to establish a reputation, thereafter to relish its effect: some were benign, some weren't. Of these, I recall with some affection a housemaster who was blessed with a distinct likeness to a monkey — something I suppose, earned by the set of his jaw, low forehead and interesting hair. Far from resenting his appearance or nickname (never used to his face), he played up to it by mannerisms in speech and posture: hand on his heart, head on one side — he was a walking mannerism, but enjoyed it all and was generally liked for it — largely because he didn't constitute a threat.

Actually Monkey's influence was more potent and long lasting than I had realised at the time; Peter and Michael Ball, the twins who later were to become my brothers-in-law, and who subsequently became bishops (with such a singular name, why not canons?), went to Lancing some years after I had left, and were in Monkey's house. Much later on family occasions, I was to become aware that in my wife's brothers, many of his characteristics lived on, not quite so much in appearance perhaps, but certainly in mannerism and tone of voice, a fascinating insight to me who had previously observed him at one remove for several years. I was pleased for Monkey, since such continuity would have appealed to his quirky sense of humour and I'm sure his legacy still sits comfortably at their ecclesiastical table.

Another member of staff, whose subject was Latin, was a very different proposition. Everything about him embodied threat: he was stocky, short in body, trousers, hair and sight — he wore incredibly thick round glasses — and shortest of all in temper. His explosions were a class act in the widest sense, and evidently something he relished. In the classroom his practice was to shuffle a pack of playing cards, having at the beginning of term allocated various numbers to individuals I was the six of hearts and diamonds and therefore known as Red Six. When it came to answering questions on vocabulary or whatever, he would shuffle the pack well aware of the tensions zinging round the room, slap a card on his desk and boom whatever question it was at the unfortunate whose card had been turned up. Failure to come up with the goods at the beginning of a lesson was tantamount to lighting a fuse that smouldered through tense minutes, until one wrong answer too many reached the powder keg. I have to say I remember him without affection, for whatever his problems, and doubtless he had many, he did much to inhibit my and others' enjoyment and understanding of Latin. Reputedly brilliant at bridge, as a teacher he was useless, a menace who should never have been allowed anywhere near a classroom.

On the other side of the coin was Moffat, I can't remember whether that was a Christian or surname, but it was what everybody called him. He was a retired clergyman who had been drafted in to teach when we arrived at Moor Park; a saintly man and looking the part, he had an unfortunate habit of calling everybody "darling", just a quirk no doubt, because I'm sure he had no physical interest in boys, or women either for that matter. Poor Moffat had an extra burden to carry as he was detailed to prepare candidates for Confirmation, a process taken particularly seriously at Lancing.

Moffat's main problem was that we were barbarians, and confirmation classes were time out from evening school and to be enjoyed. Actually to his everlasting credit, he made much of the ground to be covered interesting, but inevitably he had to come to the happily anticipated subject of sex. With delicacy he touched on such matters as adolescence and the emergence of sexuality, which inevitably brought him to the dreadful temptations to be avoided if God's Temple, as he put it, was not to be corrupted and so on. This of course brought forth those ambushing and impertinent questions that must have given many a sensitive confirmation teacher nightmares over the years — always very seriously asked with the wicked innocence of somebody who knows he has his teacher on the back foot. I'm afraid that was when class discipline tended to lapse while everybody expressed personal opinions, some very personal, and often varying considerably from the original premise. For poor saintly Moffat this must have been purgatory; I suspect he had never before been in an arena full of predators with such innocent faces circling him with their barbs and nets. He was a civilised man from a gentler background of music and attentive congregations to salve his serious mind. How he fended off such impertinences I don't recall, but somehow he did, and I think it was probably his inherent decency and obvious honesty that saved him — also perhaps, by the hard to believe fact that we weren't entirely cretinous. Order was restored after the sport had been enjoyed to the full, and reasonable discussion was resumed thereafter, but I often wonder about the doubts he must have had of any possibility of our eventual salvation.

As at Ellesmere we had variety in our classrooms, but now both staff and pupils had to adapt to an even greater range of locations varying from well-appointed and sometimes panelled rooms in the house itself — to a brass-monkey rectory attic, its windows hung with icicles as long as stalactites in winter, a room rivalled by an equally arctic disused dairy in the grounds of Moor Park itself. These were the down sides of our having to live an ad hoc life, but it didn't seem to be much of an issue at the time, particularly as staff noses dripped as much as ours — and at least our blood was thick.

An exception to the somewhat parochial locations of our lessons at Moor Park was the science laboratory situated in Ludlow Grammar School, that generously allowed us the use of their premises and which, wonderfully, were warm. Here we were introduced to the mysteries of physics and chemistry, chemistry being the better option when it didn't involve learning formulae since experiments occasionally were, so to speak, very ad hoc. I personally learned that if you added a few drops of nitric acid on to a penny, it reacted with the copper and produced pungent brown clouds of nitrous something or other. It's also a fact that if you extinguish your Bunsen burner then blow down it (let it cool first), all neighbouring Bunsens will be extinguished as well. Obviously such experiments did little to push back the frontiers of our knowledge, but used sparingly they brightened up the gloomy prospect of a long ride in the rain back to Moor Park.

CHAPTER
FIFTEEN

Don't Be Such a Baby

Schoolwork and its associated staff were one aspect of our life — another would have to be those who actually made Moor Park tick. Matrons of the time were, it seemed to me, very much of a kind: they were trained nurses from the hard school of the times, many of them of an age suggesting they had served in field stations and hospitals of the First World War; those of my experience were all spinsters or may have been widows — whichever they were, they had an unmistakable edge to them. Their uniform with that wimple-like headgear flowing back from forehead to shoulders in a starched white tide, was pretty standard; they were belted and badged and totally efficient, being quite merciless when it came to ripping a sticky bandage off a hairy leg — an action usually accompanied by exhortations like "don't be such a baby!" Hidden under that façade however, was a streak of humanity only occasionally to show itself, but was there all the same. At Moor Park our matron, Miss Taylor, had all these qualities — dispensing plasters, laxatives and good advice impartially to those in need. More than that though, she could be a bulwark against some of the worst slings and arrows of daily life — especially if she scented bullying. She had authority, knew how to use it and was never questioned.

Frank was another essential part of the running of the place and it's difficult to specify his job exactly since he appeared to have a hand in most things. He wore a short blue-striped jacket and dark trousers every day for all the years I knew him. The catering and everything else worked because he made it work, as no doubt he'd made things work at Lancing too: I remember seeing him there, keeping an eye on all the scurrying waiters at mealtimes in the big hall. He was the one who tolled the bell that shattered sleep at exactly 7 a.m., polished floors, chivvied an elderly gardener, smoked Woodbines and brooked no cheek from anyone. I never knew what he'd been before he found his berth at Lancing, but I have no doubt he'd done the business in the First World War, and I'd bet a pound to a penny he had worn a few stripes on his sleeve in the process.

I remember the food at school in those years as being remarkably good except for breakfast porridge, which was lumpy with burnt bits and horrible. I imagine it was the number of ration books available that made school catering relatively easy: Sunday lunches were always excellent in the traditional way and weekday meals were reasonable, though items like butter and sugar arrived in miniscule quantities. Bread was never rationed during the war and surely served as a morale booster as well as a filler; beer and cigarettes were often in short supply, but neither was rationed and must also have been significant in keeping up the country's spirits, since nearly everybody smoked in those days, and beer drinking was a national activity — not that any of those activities were supposed to apply to us. Perish the thought.

I must mention the girls. Monastic Lancing had no option but to import young women past school leaving age but too young for the services, into the male portals of Moor Park. Their job was to make beds, empty our chamber pots (poor things) and generally sort out our sleeping quarters after we disappeared for the day — that was done before Frank got them down to the cavernous depths of the kitchen for the washing up and another day's chores. They were paid boarders unlike us, and were ruled by Mattie who was nearly Frank's equal in authority: she had a sergeant major's glare and an unremitting watching brief over her girls' activities and safety. Their quarters and Mattie's were situated on the floor directly above ours: such proximity, but they might as well have been as distant as the stars.

Never was an area more impenetrable or more out of bounds than that heaven we imagined was waiting above us though it quite failed to inhibit ideas on how to penetrate the metaphorical barbed wire. To those of us without sisters or contact with young women, those girls might just as well have come from another planet and were seen to be disturbing creatures, giggling and provocative on the rare occasions we came face to face. What they thought of us, spotty and gauche, I hate to think. Naturally there were apocryphal tales of visits to their quarters that were much relished, but with the never-sleeping vigilance of Mattie, no prurient story was ever validated. Imagination ruled — as usual.

Chapel still featured large in our lives; a handsome panelled room near the dining hall had been rigged up with an altar and chairs, and we had evensong there every day. Actually it had a comfortable atmosphere in which to wind down, there was a picture window overlooking the lawns and field that ran down to the lake, and it felt a positively welcoming place, no doubt surprised by its elevated role in life. Every day the piano was played both imaginatively and expertly by a boy whose name was Dale, if I remember right. His most appreciated skill was to incorporate a pop tune into an ecclesiastical setting so well camouflaged that staff never noticed. We used to egg him on, not that he needed much, and at the end of evensong when staff and seniors were departing, we got the full range: it seemed delightfully wicked to enjoy a Hoagy Carmichael variation wafting through the smoke of newly extinguished altar candles. Happily, Dale was never twigged and was still at it when I became a prefect; naturally there was nothing I could do about it — tradition has to start somewhere — and in any case was supposed to be important to the smooth running of schools like ours. Dale was more than good enough to have had a musical career, but I've never heard of him since. I just hope he survived the war.

I mentioned free time on Sundays and occasionally on Saturdays as well if we weren't involved in a match. I had a friend, Tom, with whom I went ferreting in the

101

wooded country round Moor Park; mostly it was part of an estate rich in rabbits as well as gamekeepers who were too old to have gone to war. Here then was a challenge, and with luck, money to be made at the rate of 6d per rabbit paid by an enterprising Ludlow butcher who asked no questions. This was big money when I remember that Father gave me a £1 note that had to last all term. Fired with incentive, Tom and I made the most of an opportunity which, astonishingly in retrospect, was never picked-up by our housemaster or anybody else as far as I was aware. Was it ignorance or blind eye? I shall never know.

We bought our ferrets from a nearby farmer who was well disposed to us, even allowing us to work his land occasionally — though not as occasionally as he might have thought. By degrees as finances allowed, we collected our equipment together: such essentials as nets, carrying boxes for the ferrets and a spade were assembled — and autumn and winter weekends assumed a new and positive meaning. There was magic in setting off to some pre-discussed location, netting the warren holes, putting down the ferret — and waiting. We lay flat on our bellies with the old forest scents of leaf mould and earth heavy in the air, hanging on the telltale thumping that startled rabbits make before they bolt — and watchful too for gamekeepers. I learned then much of the field craft that later was to be useful to me, and recall with pleasure that special feel of old woodland fidgeting in the stillness, busy getting ready for the world of night as the light fades — a time to think about collecting our things together ready to disappear. All of it was a stage setting itself up: a worried pheasant making a fuss about the business of roosting, a fox barking somewhere close by, twigs suddenly and unaccountably snapping. Never were we more edgy and alert.

I learned about silence that's never actually silent, about shadows that move when they shouldn't move, and how to stay so still that you hardly breathe at all. We learned quickly because there was every incentive to do so, and we must have been pretty good at it, because we were never caught — though once we had to sacrifice our nets to get away. The skill was not only not to get caught by prowling gamekeepers who didn't like boys anyway, but also not to be recognised. Had we been recognised it would have become a provable school matter relentlessly to be pursued. It wouldn't have been long I suspect, before our ferrets and the equipment we kept in a disused shed down by a sawmill, would have been noticed and conclusions drawn.

We kept our ferrets snug in the dry sweet smelling sawdust we were given by the sack from the sawmill, and took pleasure in keeping them warm and comfortable, grooming their supple bodies till their coats bloomed. In the holidays we took them home in their carrying boxes, sometimes to the critical dismay of some of our fellow passengers — this was because my lad was a polecat ferret and he smelt a bit, not a bad smell at all, just his smell — and still no official notice was taken. In those strange and dangerous days the unusual tended to be regarded as commonplace.

Wartime, as we were to find out, stands accepted notions on their heads — more than a few being to our advantage.

CHAPTER
SIXTEEN

A Foot in the Other Camp

Holidays came round as usual. After that summer in Buckinghamshire I went home for holidays to Eastbourne, a town that had become a restricted area by then, but it was where my parents lived and regulations allowed me to stay there too. Father was established as an assistant manager at the Barclays Terminus Road Branch by then, and in between whiles he did his stint in the Home Guard, while Mother went off to do her canteen work for the troops stationed in and around the town.

My first holiday return to Sussex was at Christmas 1940, and it was my earliest real taste of what war at close quarters actually involved. We were staying in the Star Inn at Alfriston, a village near Eastbourne as a Christmas treat; we had snow, lots of it, which made the place pretty much the stereotype Christmas card picture, those being the days before the village became more of a gentrified country suburb. One traditional starlit night around 3a.m., a crippled Wellington bomber on its way back from a raid on Turin (as we later learned), flew low over the village and crashed near Littlington, a hamlet a mile or so distant. That was the end of a very untraditional Christmas for the unfortunate crew.

A few days later when visiting the crash site I tried, ineffectually of course, to understand what it must have been like for that crew, too low to bail out, in those moments before they disintegrated with their plane on a stretch of snowy contour often rated by guide books as a beauty spot. That something of such magnitude should happen at such a time and in such a place, which had been transformed to an area of melted snow and twisted metal — with all the dimensions that films never show — I found horrifying. In terms of realisation of the indifference of circumstance, it had much the same effect on me as that plunge into the sailing-boat pond of my early childhood — something impersonal dark and cold, though this time I was old enough to begin to realise its implications. I moved a little further away from childhood in those bleak moments.

In subsequent school holidays I found myself learning to adapt to a life with different parameters, some of which were immediate in their impact. As an occasional visitor from another world, I didn't at first have the equanimity of my parents and those like them who lived in Eastbourne all the time, but it was an exciting experience of unusual diversions which didn't take long to get used to. Eastbourne was an easy place to attack with the Messerschmidts and Focke-Wulf fighter bombers coming in low over Beachy Head, even lower over town, to drop the handy bomb slung underneath the fuselage, and scream away again before the sirens and ack-ack had time to respond. It was reckoned that these were easy training missions for novice pilots, hence the frequency of their visits.

One Sunday Father's bank in Terminus Road received one of their offerings through its green carbuncle-like dome, and for the next week or two he and other staff, plus Mother and me, were busy drying out sodden wads of banknotes that had been rescued from a wrecked and flooded strong room. The £5 banknotes which were white and much larger than other notes of the time, were partially dried then pegged out on improvised washing lines before getting a quick going over with an iron from Mother: even that didn't draw much comment, and none were stolen either. It was a lucky break that it happened on a Sunday, otherwise there'd have been nobody left — including Father — to peg anything out to dry.

The fact that Eastbourne seemed to attract a lot of unwelcome and gratuitous attention, made little difference to what we did as far as day-to-day activities were concerned. Father went off to the bank at 8.30a.m. every morning even if he'd been up Home Guarding all night; often Mother and I would go into town to shop, which meant getting what we could with our ration books, then going to have a cup of dubious coffee in the local department store, Bobby's, which somehow managed to keep going. The restaurant clung with determination to its pre-war niceties, the elderly waitresses still bustled about in their green dresses and lacy caps and aprons, depositing coffee in front of us as if the beans came straight from Mocha; sometimes there would be a discreet three-piece orchestra playing its repertoire of 1930s songs — evidently it took a lot to disturb the very foundations of a seaside tradition.

The few civilians left in town with time on their hands would home in for coffee, and eleven a.m. became something of a social occasion when the most recent events would be discussed in a matter of fact sort of way. Occasionally the local air-raid siren would sound and everybody hurried down to the basement until the "All clear" echoed its extraordinary note (it sounded like a demented cuckoo). This system was peculiar to Eastbourne because the standard warning had a habit of sounding after the raiders had gone home. It was activated by observers on Beachy Head and supposed to give an earlier warning: sometimes it did — but it was out of its league usually, because the German intruders came in too low and too fast to be spotted in time.

One morning full of coffee and gossip, Mother and I were cycling back home from town, bicycles being the only civilian transport in those days — when we became aware of a lot of machine gun and engine noise with little puffs of dust spraying off the road and flint-stone walls in front of us. I have an enduring picture of Mother diving headlong off her bike and landing in the shelter of a wall, red in the face and furious, but unscathed. Never had I parted company with a bike with greater alacrity (never had incentive been so strong), landing wetly in the detritus of a vegetable stall, which evidently had stood there for several generations. It was a messy way to get a worm's eye view of the world, but the moment passed.

There was another way of socialising in those days besides Bobby's — it was what was later to become the ubiquitous British Restaurant. The result of somebody's brilliant idea, the BR as it was called, provided lunch without the need for coupons (as far as I'm aware) — a two-course meal, a cup of tea and a relaxing break for anyone who wanted to turn up. There was a BR in the Towner Art Gallery in Eastbourne's Old Town, and this became Mother's focus; every day five days a week, she put on an overall and headscarf and ferried plates of whatever it was, usually a stew followed by a solid pudding covered with very yellow sugarless custard. It was great — a true wartime greasy spoon without the grease — and with the art gallery you had a helping of culture to go with it. On the panelled walls hung gilded paintings of *The Fighting Temaraire*, Nelson's last moments with Hardy at Trafalgar, as well as a selection of defunct local dignitaries who glumly stared while you tackled your custard. The nation-wide institution of the British restaurant was a great success: it served food and incongruity, and must have been life saving for the thousands who paid their 9d for a meal; its popularity was such that it survived for years after 1945. Best of all, it was absolutely Mother's bag: loaded with dinners and enthusiasm, she slotted effortlessly into a noisy ad hoc world light years removed from her tidy empire at home — and it was obvious she loved every minute of it.

School holidays in Eastbourne were much of a pattern and before long I had become accustomed to the contrasts they offered. Mother worked wonders with what food there was on ration, she even made whale-meat stews tasty and we never went hungry; by then we were used to minimal rations of sugar, butter and other things we take for granted today. There was of course, the "under the counter" factor: if you were a regular customer somewhere an extra something might occasionally come your way, perhaps liver or a packet of dubious suet, and that helped. We grew vegetables in our garden and Father acquired half a dozen hens which thrived on the scraps we were able to feed them.

There was a machine-gun post on the roof of a house nearly opposite us, in theory there to deal with a marauding Luftwaffe, but in practice it wasn't a lot of use since the crew spent most of their time playing cards and visitors didn't hang about. Sometimes we passed eggs up to them to keep them happy, or at least awake; it must have been a good job in summer because Eastbourne gets a lot of sun, but winters must have been a very different proposition. Did they ever fire a shot in anger? Not in my holidays, but at least our chickens weren't put off their lay by a couple of Lewis guns blasting off over their heads. I expect life would have changed for those crews when the tide of war had turned and we were on the offensive; in 1942 there was so much to come, so many lives to be lost. I hope those guys made it.

The end of holidays meant the tedious business of travelling back to Ludlow and beyond, with such treks being unpredictable and rail timetables more imaginative by the day. I usually met up with friends at Paddington for the longer part of the journey, but sometimes longer became almost infinite; one snowy evening we got as far as Hereford where we had to change trains for Ludlow; our connecting train was said to be two hours late, so we trudged round an almost deserted Hereford in search of something better than the station waiting room with its blue lighting and inhospitable seats. As we explored the desolate streets, a roof's worth of melting snow landed with awful speed just in front of us, bringing down a tile or two with it — so we took the hint and returned to the station to find our train waiting at the platform an hour or so early. Without that avalanche we'd have missed it. Guardian angel, or what?

Not that our troubles were quite over. Ludlow station was as deserted as only small country stations can be when the entire world is in bed except you. I recall looking longingly at the blacked out sleeping windows of the Feathers Hotel as we trudged up the hill from the station at the start of our three-mile hike back to Moor Park loaded with heavy cases. It seemed our eventual and very untimely arrival was not all that welcome to staff who had been waiting up — they didn't exactly say "where the bloody hell have you been?" but the sentiment was certainly there. Cocoa-less and knackered, we slipped thankfully into our damp beds. Term had started.

CHAPTER SEVENTEEN

Dad's Army... and Mumps

Once more back in country harness, I and some other seniors joined the Home Guard and became a somewhat dubious part of the Shropshire Light Infantry. By virtue of the fact I was by then head of my house, I acquired the lofty rank of sergeant in the school platoon — not a very logical arrangement but that was the way it worked. This involved occasional Sunday exercises after I had clumped up and down the aisle in army boots exacting reluctant pennies from the congregation at morning service in Richard's Castle church.

On one occasion we had been volunteered for a night guard, and were assigned the job of watching over a water pipeline that crossed the nearby River Teme. It was a night of brilliant moonlight, the river silvered and black, with Shropshire huddled under shadows and obviously harbouring a million hidden troops ready to attack. The inspecting officer turned up at around midnight coughing loudly in case we were asleep; he appeared to be something of a forerunner to Captain

Mainwaring of *Dad's Army* fame, though as gentle as Mainwaring was stroppy. Regretfully, he ordered me to turn out the guard for inspection, regarded our somewhat shambolic line without comment, warned us of the imminent probability of attack by paratroops dedicated to the idea of blowing up our pipeline over the Teme, then he dismissed us and wished me a good night. Heavy with guard commander's responsibilities, I didn't sleep for most of the night and so helped to preserve Ludlow's water supplies.

Home Guarding had other facets that I loved. In the holidays I was transferred to the Eastbourne detachment of the Royal Sussex Home Guard; I had to take off my stripes and become a private, but what the hell, and I often did night guard duty together with my Father watching a stretch of promenade from the Wish Tower to the pier; it was a surreal experience to be patrolling with a loaded rifle slung from my shoulder, along a darkened promenade that I'd so often seen full of people doing their holiday thing in deck chairs, licking ice-cream cornets and cooking in the sun. How different was that part of the front at 2a.m. in 1943 — how cold and deserted then — the beach shadowed by endless coils of barbed wire and skeletal traceries of linked steel poles set into shingle that we knew harboured countless mines. A spill of moonlight on the sea would sometimes illuminate the pier with a 50yd gap cut out of its length — it was no holiday spot any more and not much of a landing place either.

But the real fun came on Sunday mornings when we did street fighting exercises down at the Bourne Street

113

end of Eastbourne, a part of the town that had been so badly bombed that it was a shambles of wrecked houses similar to what I was to see in the advance towards Germany later on. We cleared houses of fanatical SS with much shouting, and discharging of blanks from our antiquated rifles — but the real business was when we got round to blowing things up. The resident explosives genius was Sergeant Jelly, a large and happy man who taught us about fuses and what you do and don't do with explosive charges — and then we blew them up. We learned to pack a drainpipe with thunder flashes, an army version of a 5 November squib — then project missiles like imitation mortars, a system that worked amazingly well unless the drainpipe disintegrated. After a satisfying morning session we packed up and went home to Sunday lunch and a quiet afternoon.

Those were strange formative and vivid times for me, moments of occasional near-vertical learning curves: but in retrospect I realise how relatively safe and comfortable they were when compared with the lives of young people in occupied Europe. I suppose incongruity was the name of the game; there were days that might include the totally mundane and the far from ordinary, pretty well at the same time. At home we slept without comment under a Morrison steel table in our dining room, often listening to the grumbling roar of the Luftwaffe on its way to London — to doze fitfully until they returned, once to dump a load of incendiaries on the Downs between us and the sea as a parting bonus — and then around 6a.m. we would hear the milkman and the clink of bottles on the doorstep.

I had mumps under those conditions huddled in a chair in the kitchen before being shoved under that table, a piece of non-furniture you just didn't need to bang your head on, as I found out. Mumps turned out to be a hideous complaint: I wanted to eat but couldn't because of the pain when I salivated.

"Mumps is bad for your testicles," our jokey doctor told me, "so if you want to stamp your mark on the world, don't mess about now." Whatever did he mean? My parents took such gratuitous advice seriously, and I was incarcerated as well as starving for most of the holidays.

Stuck between the extraordinary and the every day made the whole experience of living in two worlds even more interesting as time went on. People living in Eastbourne all the time took most things in their stride, but for me it was the novelty factor that emphasised the difference between a quiet bit of poaching in remote Shropshire — and the sudden appearance of a German fighter-bomber making a very low pass straight at me (it seemed) while I was on an errand to the post office in Eastbourne's Old Town. I discovered then that there's a big difference between watching such things on film and actually gawping at a real bomb whistling overhead, to explode in somebody's garden a few hundred yards away. It did little for my equilibrium at the time, even less for the unfortunate recipient's rockery and windows, but it was at least an incident I was able to exaggerate at school to disbelieving friends who'd heard it all before.

News, which we seldom missed, came over the radio at 6p.m. as it had always done; usually read by Alvar Liddell's familiar voice, it made the best of not very encouraging material. The Dieppe raid in 1941 gave us some idea of the reality of things. For weeks before the assault, Eastbourne had been full of Canadian troops and tanks and everyone knew something was brewing — doubtless the Germans did as well. One morning the town was empty of troops, most of whom were destined not to return from Dieppe, and next day the sky was full of our fighters heading for France.

Scenting something interesting I biked from home, sweating up the horribly steep Sanatorium Hill that takes you to the seaward side of the Downs where a number of emergency landing strips for damaged planes had been established along the flat areas just in from the chalk cliffs. These had always interested me, as they seemed to be places poised and ready for something exciting to happen, with a Nissen hut or two and a discreet windsock to add to the atmosphere. They were strategically placed to give landing space to a pilot nursing home a damaged Spitfire or Hurricane, also — and important to me — they were usually unmanned so you weren't likely to get chivvied away if you hung about hoping for something to happen.

On that particular day it wasn't long before the fighters began to return, having given support to the Canadians vainly trying to give Dieppe a hard time; most flew straight over back to their airfields, but soon I was watching a lone Hurricane late and limping along just above cliff level with a lot of its tail-plane missing.

Those airstrips really were a life-saving idea and this pilot made it safely down, bouncing and chuntering over the springy turf. I desperately wanted to run over and talk to him, but somehow had wit enough to know he'd probably be in no mood to talk to anyone — least of all to a gormless schoolboy — but that must have more than made the day for him, certainly it did for me. Very late and big with news, I burned back down Sanatorium Hill bursting with exaggerated accounts of how close I'd been to a damaged Hurricane — practically in it in fact. Those holidays were never boring.

I believe the years of 1939 to 1945 represented the first conflict to involve civilians on a national scale, this time exposing them to death and injury in enormous numbers; the paradox is that this exposure appeared to increase morale and determination to continue life as normally as possible. I don't doubt that Germany's civilians reacted in much the same way when subjected to the RAF's thousand bomber raids on their cities; it follows really, personal survival and the fundamental needs to stay alive, keep warm and eat as well as possible, concentrate the mind — probably to the near exclusion of everything else. What I saw in Eastbourne was just a microcosm of a much greater whole: people living as civilians in a town that had more than its share of sharp-edge warfare, reacting with an attitude both resigned and sanguine, plus a very definite contempt for all things German. Fear was a factor, but one of many.

Another aspect of war indiscriminately aimed at civilians was the appearance of the V1 — the "Flying Bomb" in the skies over southeast England late in the war. Launched from sites in Holland and the channel coast, they were aimed at London, though as a terror weapon, pretty well anywhere would have done. The heart-stopping thing about them was the rasping note of their engines — you only had to hear it once — never to forget. The engine stopped when fuel ran out, and never was a silence so profound as the one that followed when that buzz ceased . . . roulette seconds . . . the wheel spinning — little ball bouncing round its numbers as the bomb descended — to explode . . . not on your number this time. Occasionally a patrolling fighter pilot would fly close enough to tip the missile off course, a delicate wing-to-wing nudge sufficient to send it back in the direction it came from.

Daylight air activity in those days wasn't all one-way however, and later on in the war American raids on continental targets intensified. One summer Sunday afternoon the sky was filled by a great formation of American Flying Fortress bombers, which were flown concentrated in blocks of maybe 100 planes so their fire against enemy fighters could be coordinated, concentrated, and thus made more effective. Flying their tight formation, these bombers were escorted by Mustang fighters with their cut-off wingtips and unmistakeable engine note, which were patrolling the flanks of the main force — seeming tiny in contrast to the bombers. Tragically, one of the fighters, perhaps caught in turbulence, flew too close and collided with one of the

Fortresses — immediately there was a great flash, the fighter disappeared and the Fortress began a flaming descent to the sea: one parachute . . . two . . . three . . . appeared and opened while we waited for more — but they were the only ones. We didn't see the bomber hit the sea, but heard the impact. Within minutes the Eastbourne lifeboat and its amazing crew were out there picking up the survivors — three out of a crew of seven, I believe. The rest of the armada closed up the gap and flew on to its target.

CHAPTER
EIGHTEEN

Getting Involved

After holidays like that, school and Shropshire came as a major anti-climax, which took a while to shrug off at the beginning of each term but there were some compensations. As a prefect I took my meals at the headmaster's table during my last couple of terms, one of many advantages that put a different complexion on school life; as one of the six school prefects, you made things happen rather than have things happen to you. You were given authority and were expected to use it properly, another element in a full life — and I enjoyed doing things my way for a change.

Towards the end of term that summer, I with a few others were given permission to sleep out on the roof of the house, a not very sheltered flat area surrounded by a balustrade. Sleeping outside in deep country for the first time on a night flecked with a suggestion of rain, became for me a theatre of movement and echoes of history, of imagination's raiding parties — shadows down from the Marches, soft with Welsh expletives, on their way to transfix Ludlow — while, as I watched, fifty miles away came the flaring medley and faint dumps of sound as Birmingham was fired again by the

Luftwaffe — two histories, one in the making. The lake where we sometimes fished for roach and perch was floating a fragment of moon — and in the ambushing shadows of woodland beyond, came once, shockingly, the jarring cut-off scream of some hunted prey. And I — that smallest thing, from under a blanket on a knobbly mattress, felt blitzed by apprehensions I hadn't felt before — witness to the sheer scale of things in a world where circumstance rules, a realisation taking me another step closer to adulthood. Sleep did not come easily that night.

While I battled with academe I was always beset with the niggling worry that the war might be over before I could get to it. Such innocence, and something I was to unlearn pretty quickly when the time came. It was a symptom of the age of course, brave days of Churchill's rhetoric and everybody's unquestioning certainty that military defeat wasn't on the cards: all that being an amalgam of the results of tradition and propaganda in a nation that had dug itself in. Coupled with that must have been the mindset propagated by schools like Lancing — the whole set up from beginning to end being "My Country, right or wrong", with an armoury and military training to back it up. The fact that wars create more problems than they solve and cost millions of everything, was a notion much less in evidence then than it's just beginning to be today; it was small wonder that people like myself couldn't get involved quickly enough.

At long last the time came, and late in 1943 my friend Tom and I were given a day off school to go to

Hereford and enlist in the army. As we cycled the three miles or so to Ludlow Station early enough for the top of Clee Hill still to be shrouded in mist, it seemed much more than just a welcome escape from the usual routine — it was a closing of a chapter in our lives which had become increasingly frustrating as we fretted for the opportunity to go and fight before the war was over — because then the tide was turning, and the much talked about "second front" in France was on the cards.

The timing of enlistment as far as I was concerned, was partly to ensure I didn't get conscripted for the mines and become a Bevan Boy to hew truckloads of coal — not that I had anything but respect for such unsung heroes who worked in darkness a mile underground and got their lungs ruined — with little thanks from anyone. But bullshit seemed preferable to coal dust, and if you volunteered before being called up, the coal dust possibility didn't arise. I had previously optimistically flirted with the idea of training to be a pilot in the RAF, but knew my maths was not good enough — and I had never contemplated ground crew as an option. Father had been a tank man in 1917 and had fought at Cambrai, so a lot more realistically I settled for the family connection and ground action instead.

We were received at the recruiting office by an archetypal sergeant major with a rooster's strut and waxed moustache on which you could have spiked half a dozen pancakes. After all information about us had been noted down in at least triplicate, we had a medical

— for which we waited a long draughty time naked and apprehensive in a room full of cubicles; the doctor who regarded us in much the same manner as a butcher might contemplate a pen of cattle, sounded our chests, gripped our testicles none too gently and told us to cough. That was standard practice we learned, but I still wonder what nugget of information about my health he gleaned from it.

Our next hurdle was a series of intelligence tests — pages of strange squiggles to make something of — apparently requiring skills far removed from our usual classroom efforts. I remember glancing across at Tom who cast his eyes heavenwards and it was comforting to know that I wasn't the only idiot. I think we had about half an hour of that, before our papers were collected for "processing" as the clerk ominously informed us — somehow managing to convey the likelihood of dire consequences if we really were as stupid as we looked.

In the meantime we had an interview with a gloomy major who warned us of the dangers, as he put it, of dallying with women — a shortcoming that apparently did nothing for the war effort: it was a point I privately considered debatable even in those early days — morale after all, is crucial. Isn't it? After that we had to sign numerous papers and swear allegiance to the King — all of us disappointed that there was no "King's Shilling" being offered to recruits, it seemed a bit mean somehow when pocket money was, even with ferreting funds, always in short supply.

And that if I remember right, was that. We were fit, apparently OK in the intelligence department, as we hadn't been among those recalled for more excursions into the world of intelligence testing (somewhat to our surprise) — and had been warned about women. Who could want more? We were now intelligent men walking tall into the nearest pub; the landlord looked us up and down as we leaned nonchalantly against the bar.

"What might you young gents be wanting?" he enquired, putting a final polish on a glass, "lemonade?"

"We've just enlisted in the army' we replied indignantly."

"Ah, that's different then" he replied, "I thought you were just schoolboys chancing your luck." and he pulled us a couple of dark half pints. "That'll do to be starting with", he remarked, and watched us struggle with the stuff with the faintest of grins. We weren't used to beer and it tasted horrible — but we got it down somehow. A rite of passage maybe.

We didn't hurry back to school. Being perpetually hungry, we hunted around and discovered a teashop that was still traditional with its chintzy curtains and sampler on a wall — and, amazingly, still in business. A taciturn waitress eventually produced a couple of aptly named rock cakes and a pot of pallid tea — which, if nothing else, helped to clear the taste of beer from our mouths. After that we spent some time in the ancient silence of the cathedral, deserted except for the figure of a black-gowned verger pottering among the choir stalls like an elderly bird.

I had half hoped for a look at the famous Mappa Mundi — that remarkable creation that put Jerusalem at the centre of the world, and which was usually kept in the cathedral — but the verger told us that it had been removed to a place less likely to be the target of enemy bombs. On a less exalted level we sniggered at a gargoyle that bore a close resemblance to our most disliked Latin master, and left the lovely place feeling refreshed.

Our train back to Ludlow was late, about par for the course in days when timetables had little to do with reality — but we didn't mind because it had been a day out of school, and the world had changed for us. There was much to think about as we trundled back through sleepy countryside, to a life that wasn't going to be the same for much longer — to me that prospect tasted good. We had moved a step closer.

CHAPTER
NINETEEN

Getting Nearer Getting Real

Ludlow itself was a salve to my impatience. I loved the place and still do; even now when I go back it's still possible to recognise parts of it that have changed little in the sixty or so years since we used to bomb through it on our way to the playing fields on the far side of town. Cycling back muddy and noisy, we would stop in at our favourite watering hole, De Gray's, a café that's still there virtually unchanged today. They were very tolerant of us, but since we consumed vast quantities of their dried egg on toast and anything else they had on offer, it must have been a good mutual relationship. Dried egg, about the only eggs you saw in those days, was vividly yellow and pre-scrambled: we thought it delicious and kept us going just long enough to bike back to school for supper.

The town is perched on a hill with the River Teme keeping its feet cool on the southern side, and it was a great hill for cyclists in those virtually traffic-free days. Going uphill to De Gray's kept you fit, if breathless — because it seemed endless and near vertical towards the top. But afterwards, afterwards — full of dried egg and steam came the awful delight of going flat out down that lovely drop, through the archway that squeezes the road to egg timer shape for a dark 20yds (don't meet anything coming the other way there) with wind whistling, tyres humming — to fly down and over the river Teme's ancient bridge, collecting enough momentum to get you up the other side to where the road flattens out on its way back to school. Lunatic? Certainly. Irresponsible? Completely. Accidents? None.

Ludlow itself had attractions other than its hill. In summer you could hire a boat and mess about on the river, keeping an eye on the weirs, or take the bikes at speed down a risky line of steps that formed part of the path along the high ground of the cliffs on the opposite side of the river to the town itself. The place also boasted a couple of cinemas, though they were usually out of bounds; but on one occasion there was a showing of a film called *Birth of a Baby* and remarkably the headmaster lifted the cinema prohibition and allowed us to see the film. Never I suspect, has a cinema done so well on a couple of afternoons, its seats filled with absorbed voyeurs; it was another small step in our self-appointed task of unravelling one of life's ongoing mysteries.

We didn't have half-term holidays and speech days but Lancing had, and no doubt still has, Saints' days — the names of which I'm ashamed to say I can't remember. Apart from morning chapel, these were days off when you were free to do whatever you wanted within the limits of time and reason. When Tom and I weren't ferreting we explored; bikes were the instruments of our liberation, and often we covered a lot of miles on roads usually empty of motor traffic except for an occasional army truck or farm vehicle. We discovered places like Presteign, Kington, Knighton and Clun in the lovely border country of the Marches — but you needed to be fit because these rides involved the kind of hills that are vertical and go on for ever. Once we tried to get to Shrewsbury, but it was too far even for us.

Apart from my Buckinghamshire summer in 1940, Shropshire was my first taste of deep country that had remained much the same in essence for centuries. Yuppies and the dreaded green wellies were still decades away, village houses still had outside privies together with a cold water tap in the kitchen, and a lot of what we saw in reality, we find today in Olde Worlde calendars and Christmas cards. Progress as it's called, had seen to the surface of many of the roads, and I remember the comfortable hum of our tyres on tarmac as Shropshire slipped by; if you met anything on a blind corner it was likely to be a leisurely horse and cart, or very occasionally an ancient tractor stinking of paraffin with a crank handle sticking out of its front. In summer it was otherworld country, remote, silent, and heavy with the myriad scents of farmyards, hedgerow flowers and mown hayfields. In winter the cloud lowered from over the Welsh hills and its rain was the wettest I've ever encountered, dripping icily off nose and oilskins onto our knees — and the wind was always against us. But for me, either in summer or winter, the country as I explored it in those safe protected days was totally beautiful.

Maybe they weren't completely protected days. One night we received a surplus bomb donated by the Luftwaffe on its way back from attacking Liverpool or somewhere. It dropped in our ferreting woods about half a mile away with a bang that shook the whole place and provided a talking point that lasted for weeks. Next morning the crater still smoked and reeked with many trees carrying new scars, splintered and resinous — so even our part of rural Shropshire had its taste of aerial warfare. Since it wasn't my first bomb I felt mildly superior, but that time I kept it to myself, it wouldn't have gone down well with my friends, who doubtless had more than enough of my tedious holiday stories.

At about this time the headmaster's daughter, who was at university, appeared occasionally to join us for meals at the top table. I have already mentioned the effect of women on a houseful of prurient boys accustomed only to the headmaster's secretary with her spectacular knock-knees, and the girls who dwelt so tantalisingly above us — so it wasn't surprising her appearance at meals caused more than passing interest. A poised and elegant Mary walked with a pert bosom and significant roll of hip, her glossy hair pulled back into a spinsterish bun — though there was little of potential spinster about her. Unlike the headmaster's secretary who obviously didn't like boys, especially in large numbers, Mary evidently did — and usually made her entrance a little late at mealtimes, an entrance followed every step by a hundred yearning eyes and a sigh like a breeze through a cornfield. It was Bennett of course, who before long added a new dimension to that ever-popular topic: doing a passable Confucius voice despite his still rich Sussex burr, he remarked: "Wise man seeking beautiful bride should look long at bride's mother." At the next meal we looked long and hard at mother and found the thought illuminating.

There were many things to do as the end of my last term approached, one of them being the urgent matter of finding an alternative life for our ferrets — something of a problem, as the farmer who sold them to us didn't want them back since he had more than enough already, and unfortunately there were no other potential ferreters in school who we trusted enough to let them take on our lads. Tom and I agonised about this for weeks — and in the end we took them to a part of our hunting grounds that was particularly well populated by rabbits, and let them go. The last I saw of Oscar was his back end disappearing down a hole, to be greeted almost immediately by the thumping of a startled rabbit — a thumping that ceased abruptly. It seemed an almost surreal moment, a symbolic ending of a phase of my life, and I hated to leave him behind. But at least he wasn't going to go short of food, he was fit and strong, and I hoped he'd enjoy his freedom as much as I had in those Shropshire years.

Those Moor Park years offered me a new beginning, allowing the space I needed to take stock of the world and myself — and I was doubly lucky to have had the interweaving experience of school holidays in Eastbourne to give an edge to my experience of the times. When I climbed into the rickety station bus early on that last morning, I was still as green as grass — a fact that was to be emphasised before very much longer, but I think I had begun to grow an identity as well as a sense of knowing where to look for answers. And for that I was grateful.

CHAPTER
TWENTY

Not Quite the Shilling
— Or Maybe Not

It was cold and wet when I arrived at Maryhill Barracks in Glasgow complete in my Home Guard uniform, which after a long night's travelling did little to enhance my hopes of looking the smart young soldier on his way to save his country. I was not well received — explicitly not well received, and within a very short time was at the barbers being shorn of most of what I had left after having had a haircut before I started out. This was the basic training time that everybody suffered, when the corners were knocked off bloody civilians like us before they could become soldiers.

And basic it was. Several times each day we were marched back and forth across a parade ground the size of Salisbury Plain; we were cursed and screamed at by corporals, usually from a range of about 6ins, and even more loudly by the sergeant, a snarling little man whose boots and brasses dazzled the sun. When we weren't being drilled we did everything at the double, and I do mean everything. We were pumped full to overflowing with a great variety of serums and vaccinations, always with blunt needles; one needle per 100 men was the general impression, with recipients fainting in droves. Such were the effects of the shots we'd received after one nasty session, we actually were given some time off to recover, particularly from exceedingly sore arms. That afternoon several of us went to the cinema and sitting one seat apart from each other, we watched a delectable close-cropped Ingrid Bergman bring Hemingway's *For Whom the Bell Tolls* to life — the title's irony not occurring to me at the time.

When we weren't being screamed at or punctured with blunt needles, we took various guns to bits and put them together again blindfold, threw live grenades, and fired rifles and Bren guns on the ranges — about the only thing I enjoyed in those long weeks. Glasgow was large and wet, with Sauchiehall Street littered every evening with legless drunken sailors on leave from Atlantic convoy duties; one way and another I was not alone in disliking Glasgow — and Maryhill Barracks in particular.

We were a pretty mixed bunch of recruits, and doubtless the corporals and sergeant stuck with us had much to complain about. Among our numbers was an unfortunate lad who obviously wasn't quite the shilling, as they say. He had problems with just about everything: concepts like the difference between left and right were well beyond him, always to the sergeant's vocal despair, and the poor fellow's kit was usually the one that got hurled across the barrack room on kit inspections. Barrack room and kit inspections

133

loomed large in our lives, they happened every second Friday if I remember right; this meant that in any available time on a previous Thursday evening, the place was a worried hive of activity. The floor had to be burnished to ice-rink brilliance and no speck of dust could hide anywhere — but that was just a taste of the real thing, kit. Spit and polish is no misnomer, you spat on and polished your boots for hours — especially the toecaps — to a brilliant lustre with dusters and the handle of a toothbrush that never saw a tooth (have you ever "boned-up" on anything? That's where the expression must come from, surely). Anything brass was Brassoed to within an inch of its life, webbing was Blancoed, battledress pressed to razor edges everywhere. I hate to think how much Wellington's soldiers had to polish with all their buttons but at least webbing that required Blanco hadn't been invented then. Or had it?

In the morning well before the beastly bugle squawked the world awake, your bed got the treatment: blankets were folded to the last millimetre of exactitude; all kit including highly polished aluminium mess tins, were laid out on your mattress in the required manner; some keen or terrified souls got it all done the night before and then slept on the floor. Precisely at zero hour, an officer accompanied by the sergeant and sundry corporals, would appear rather in the manner of Assyrians (without their purple and gold) descending like wolves on our fold. In a deafening silence the wolves moved from bed to bed in absorbed and minute inspection of each layout. The best moment of every fortnight was when they reluctantly moved on, after what seemed several hours of study, from your patch to the next. You were off the hook. Blankets and equipment found to be less than perfect in all respects, was distributed at speed in small parcels at varying altitudes around the room, and the unfortunate owner would be giving the cooks a hand with their potatoes for several evenings.

That as I've mentioned, is where poor old Not-Quite-The-Shilling often featured large, but his real moment of glory came at the grenade-throwing exercise. Grenades are tricky things and the army had a drill for handling them as it had for practically everything else. You stand sideways to the target with the left hand forefinger through the ring that pulls out the pin holding the safety clip in place (the army always assumes you're right handed when it comes to throwing things). When you've done that, you keep a firm right hand grip on the grenade casing to prevent the clip from springing off and activating the explosive charge: activation gives you either three or five seconds grace depending on fuse setting, to dispose of the lethal thing.

When it came to Not-Quite-The-Shilling's turn, he managed all those preliminaries satisfactorily, smartly pulled out the pin as instructed — paused as if in thought — and then dropped the grenade. The sergeant in charge emitted a scream that was most certainly heard in Edinburgh, before appearing at full gallop round the corner of the bomb-throwing sap with Not-Quite-The-Shilling a couple of paces behind him, evidently thinking that this was all part of the exercise.

Luckily for him he had just cleared the corner which was at right angles to us, before the grenade exploded. That was an unexpected entertainment that had to be kept firmly locked inside our heads as the sergeant was in no mood to share the joke; handing us over to a slightly bemused corporal, he took Not-Quite-The-Shilling by the collar and hustled him away, never to be seen again. I like to think the lad was immediately promoted and given a desk at the War Office. Another scenario however, and one which didn't occur to us at the time, was that he might have been working his ticket — that is, trying to get his army discharge through well-performed acts of total incompetence at everything military — so it could have been the rest of us who were not-quite the shilling ones. Now there's a thought.

After a week or so I was interviewed to see what I was going to do to bring Hitler to his knees. The interviewing officer noted with approval the fact I was a volunteer wanting to do tanks, heard about Father's last war tank service and evidently put down all the right things, because a few weeks later I was posted to the Royal Armoured Corps for training at Bovington Camp in Dorset, where Father had done his tank training in 1916. And so at the eventual end of the mandatory six weeks, and armed with my precious rail pass, I made my way to Dorset where the tanks lived. I have since heard that Maryhill Barracks was eventually demolished, and now provides foundations for some new development. I call that progress.

CHAPTER
TWENTY-ONE

Tanks and Virgins

At Bovington Camp — what a change! After the dustcart comes the Lord Mayor's show, to reverse a cliché. The first thing to happen was an issue of the prized black berets, a battle honour conferred by the French on the British tank regiments of the First World War, and worn only by tank troops until after the Second World War.

"Drop those bloody things in the bin," ordered the quartermaster looking at our khaki forage caps in disgust. With pristine berets and the red and yellow RAC shoulder flashes for our tunics, we walked tall.

The next job was to make us throw up. To be considered for tank crew you can't, for obvious reasons, be travelsick — and before long we were taken out in pairs over the tank runs, our first introduction to the mind-numbing movement of a Sherman tank flat out over rough ground in the hands of a very experienced driver. Those drivers really took their mission seriously, trying everything to make us sick — and with some success judging by the state of the turret floor when my turn came. Inside the turret of a 30+ ton Sherman at speed over rough ground, is not the most comfortable way to travel until you learn its foibles: everything everywhere is, at best, unyielding — my first experience of the fact that there's little in a tank that's not sharp, heavy or awkward: that stopped me worrying about being sick — focusing only on clinging to something that wasn't going to bite me. That way I was so fully occupied by hope of survival that I didn't even think of anything else, finishing up bruised and breathless, but with my breakfast still inside me, and so made the grade for crew training.

The purpose of our training was to make each member of a crew able efficiently to do the work of anyone else in the tank when necessary, and that was what we did for most of the time. On Sunday mornings though, we had to endure the CO's church parade. This involved standing in immaculate ranks and best battledress on the parade ground for a very long time while the regimental band, glossy with brass and bullshit, went through an endless repertoire of stirring hymn tunes. I learned from the muted offerings of my companions some interesting and original variations on the words of many of the hymns I'd previously belted out at Lancing — variations which undoubtedly would have brought more than a frown to the brow of my former headmaster. Given suitable encouragement, I can still render most of those gems to this day.

During the next six weeks or so, we sweated our way to a good speed at the Morse code (something I never actually used) and delved into the intricacies of tank radio with its twiddles, nets and knobs. After that came the much more physical and entertaining driving and maintenance training — a course which involved, among a lot of other things, learning to replace broken or displaced tracks — usually in specially chosen near-impossible conditions. The best part though, was getting the hang of driving the apparently unstoppable weight of uncompromising metal over the long and sometimes tortuous tank runs around the camp; I loved the sheer crude presence of those beasts and the sense of speed you got at a flat-out 30mph — that seemed like 60mph — as tank-worn Dorset flashed past.

When we were judged competent, we drove out on public roads. I remember taking my tank up the very steep hill leading to Corfe Castle, a climb that has a sharp right hand corner about halfway up: now that was interesting, and it became even more absorbing on the way down when another trainee was driving. At that point gravity was with us, which wasn't much of an asset since steel tracks slide with happy abandon on tarmac given half a chance. How that dreaded corner was, should we say, barely achieved in a kind of heavy two-track drift, made me wonder if it was a good idea even to be inside the frisky beast, it was a long way to the bottom of the hill.

At about that stage in our training I had a rude taste of the reality involved in living with tanks; we were out on a night-training exercise, and at one point our convoy had pulled up for a tea break and a torchlight inspection of our equipment. Wilkinson, our driver, was at the back of the tank checking the engine, when for some unaccountable reason, the tank ahead of us started up and backed very smartly into our front —

the impact pushed us back, knocking down Wilkinson who had no chance of getting out of the way — and then completed the job by running over his leg. Luckily for him, if you can quote luck in such circumstances, he was caught between the track and the relatively soft ground of the verge, but it was still 30 tons on top of him. Miles, a friend of mine and I, found ourselves digging frantically, first with bare hands, then with makeshift spades. Under the tank there was very little space, which decreased as it slowly settled, making the work by torchlight urgent as well as stinky with poor old Wilkinson's vomit. We literally had to tunnel him out, digging along the outside of his leg and then slowly and gently underneath, until the limb was in a shallow trench with the track supported on either side by verge alone — only then could we pull him out. It seemed to take forever, and he was unconscious by the time he was loaded into an ambulance — which was just as well. For me, that experience was salutary: up to then I think I'd regarded war as a kind of sophisticated game — but never again after that night. I'd grown up a lot.

In the six months or so our intake spent at Bovington, we had a couple of forty-eight hour weekend passes out of camp, and on one of these Miles and I went off to the not so bright lights of Bournemouth to refresh our souls and bodies — particularly bodies. By then we'd become so steeped in an army life that keeps you on the move all day every day, that Bournemouth seemed initially like "dead-end ville", though to my eye it had something in common with Eastbourne. But Bournemouth had, still has no

140

doubt, a notable characteristic of its own: a strange soporific quality like nowhere else I've visited, and the result was that we slept most of the time, blearily to awake, take in an occasional meal, then drowse off again. It was not at all what we'd planned, as we were going to hit town in a big way. I'd even contemplated the thought of trying my luck with an obliging ATS, which would have been my first endeavour. But it wasn't to be, we hardly got out of bed — the wrong sort of bed at that — and we both continued to be frustratingly celibate.

Back in harness, we were transferred from Bovington to Lulworth Camp on the coast, where the gunnery ranges were, and still are, situated. Having got to grips with such mysteries as breech blocks and firing pins associated with the Sherman's armament, we proceeded to do untimely damage to a lovely sweeping bank of Downs, across which a mock-up tank on rails scuttled backwards and forwards doing its best to avoid our missiles. There was much to learn and the course was intensive, with regular tests on what we were supposed to have taken in during each week: these you had to pass if you hoped to make it to the next week's instalment — and ultimately tank crew.

I also learned during the course of our final tests, not to touch a very hot shell case newly ejected from the breech after firing — this one raised a blister the size of the palm of my hand and went on burning horribly for hours. But apart from that stupidity, the spell at Lulworth was pleasant enough, and sometimes when we were off duty we went down to the cove and pottered about on a beach that wasn't infested with mines. It was a lovely spot that had been a much frequented holiday spot in peacetime, and we enjoyed digging around for fossils, skimming flat stones on the sea and forgetting about guns for a while.

As a finale to our less technical activities, we were then embarked on what was called "Dismounted Training". The Royal Armoured Corps, unlike the Royal Tank Regiment (which has no outside connections and is most likely is thankful for it), is made up of former cavalry regiments, so its vernacular and practice are based on cavalry tradition: thus we mounted and dismounted our tanks, operated in troops and squadrons. Even today I understand a tank commander in the Royal Scots Greys will order his driver to "walk on" — well he would, wouldn't he? Among other things, this particular phase of training required us to live as crew with our tanks out on the heath for a few days doing exercises such as mending tracks, and generally getting used to the things we would be expected to cope with when our world got real. Other activities involved rushing through mock-up houses, shouting and firing Sten guns at wooden pop-up Nazis — and when we'd done that satisfactorily, we were shown a few interesting ways to kill without weapons.

Actually the physical side of training had earlier on been sneakily slipped into our technical activities in the form of an occasional twenty-mile forced march, just to keep us from getting too fat and lazy I suppose. These excursions required you to march at a very fast light infantry pace (140 to the minute, I think) for half a mile or so, then we had to break into a double for the next half mile. Strangely, I found it a big relief to be doubling, and the painful bit happened each time we reverted to marching at the infantry pace — so it seemed I wasn't cut out to be an infantryman. On each occasion a truck would follow at a discreet distance, ready to pick up anybody whose feet had dropped off. As our training progressed, so these outings increased, until it was pretty well a weekly event and doubtless we were being groomed for the ultimate aspects of dismounted training.

That ultimate phase produced a *pièce de resistance* planned to complete our physical training; no, actually there were two such events. The first was to learn the official way to evacuate a burning tank under fire — live fire too, with some joker with a Bren gun shooting very close over our bewildered heads. At the appropriate moment somebody let off a smoke canister next to the tank, shouting something from his script like: "Evacuate your vehicle!" What bullshit! The exercise must have been dreamed up by wizards who'd never been near a burning tank, let alone in one; the drill itself required — before evacuation of course — the removal of the main gun's firing pin, a fiddly job at the best of times, and we were mildly surprised that a quick tidy up with dustpan and brush wasn't included in the master plan. There's only one way to bail out of a tank in that condition, as we learned, and that's fast, otherwise you get to be crisped-up like Kentucky fried chicken. The only one to gain any mileage out of this pantomime must have been the Bren gunner, who evidently occupied himself by seeing how close over our heads he could shoot without actually hitting anybody.

The other exercise really demonstrated the peak of authority's imagination. It required you to walk up a steeply inclined plank to a height of about 12ft, then to continue, helpfully encouraged by jolly corporals assembled for the sport, along the now horizontal plank for about 20ft, and then jump without hesitation off the end — our instructor was particularly keen about the no hesitation bit. That had to be accomplished wearing a greatcoat, full pack and carrying a rifle — the only time I touched a rifle for the rest of the war. Not surprisingly, this exercise gave rise to some difficulties: participants weren't at all keen on starting at the bottom of the plank let alone walking off the other end, and there were protestations and exhortations — as well as broken ankles in profusion to accommodate the waiting ambulance. From up there terra firma seemed — and was — a very long way down, though I didn't look down twice. At that point I had the fatalistic thought that a spell in hospital might at least be a bit of a rest, so I just walked off the end, hit the ground, and rolled in the approved manner, losing my rifle in the process, and stood up with world and applauding audience revolving teasingly around me. Miraculously I was intact, physically anyway. God and the army move in mysterious ways.

After all that — the fun and hard graft, the bullshit and fruitless chatting-up of ATS girls who never offered so much as a glimpse of khaki knickers, those of us who escaped concussion or broken bones, went home on embarkation leave with dreams of glory to come.

CHAPTER
TWENTY-TWO

Chasing the Rainbow

The first time I eventually left our territorial waters, was by courtesy of a tank landing craft in a convoy of such vessels out of Harwich and heading for where the action was. Flat-bottomed and welded instead of being riveted together, we bounced from wave to wave creaking and protesting in an intimidating manner, which made us edgy as welded ships had a reputation for breaking vital bits in heavy seas. Off the end of a mile-long Southend Pier, our engines broke down and we were left to wallow unhappily on our own for a couple of days while repairs were attempted. The sea was choppy to rough, and we spent much of the time making sure the tanks were shackled down effectively: a loose Sherman on a bouncing landing craft was thought to be even less of a good idea than the proverbial loose cannon.

Every time the tide turned, Southend wilfully changed its position, off the port side at breakfast, then back to the starboard at around midday. Knowing a little about tides from my childhood beach days, I soon figured out the reason for that unsettling movement of town and pier, but to those of my companions who hadn't got further than the pond in their local park, it was an intimidating phenomenon boding little good for an uncertain future. A lot of resonant labour apparently involving the frequent and prolonged use of heavy naval hammers was expended on our ship's engines, which eventually were persuaded into reluctant life. As we were about to leave a brooding Southend and its pier, a shaft of sunlight turned a passing squall into a glorious rainbow, which arched beautifully far out from land before its colours slowly faded. Thus encouraged, the Navy raised anchor from an irritable sea, and without further incident we chugged next day onto a cluttered beach with neither ice-cream man nor Punch and Judy there to greet us.

The campaign was well under way by the time we splashed ashore, but I had only to wait a few hours at the Armoured Reinforcement Unit before finding myself in the back of a truck on my way to a part of the world that appeared to be getting increasingly noisy by the minute. I had been interviewed by a recruiting major from the Sherwood Rangers Yeomanry (sometimes known as the Shitty Sherwoods), a man who wore a very lived-in face and who appeared to be a good deal older than anybody else I'd come across, so that I wondered unkindly whether somehow he'd got himself into the wrong war. After his pipe was finally ignited satisfactorily, our interview got going through a haze of St Bruno; he appeared to be mostly interested in my school — in particular by the puzzling fact that Lancing actually played soccer rather than rugby. However, that possible shortcoming appeared not to have jeopardised my suitability to join what he assured me was a regiment with more combat experience than any other to date. I wondered whether that was offered as a recommendation, but didn't ask.

Subsequently I learned the sobriquet "Shitty Sherwoods" had been donated by a regular regiment in our brigade (not a common territorial outfit like us), one where "spit and polish" was a big thing. Even more subsequently I heard that this same fashionable regiment (mentioning no names) had lost pretty near a squadron of crewless tanks which had been parked cosily along a village street somewhere or other — knocked-off like a line of coconuts by a marauding Tiger tank on its way home after a night out. Where were the crews? Polishing their brasses, I shouldn't wonder. "Their colonel," I hear you ask — "did he get a knighthood as well as a bowler hat?" I never heard, but nothing would surprise me.

Dumped in a leaguer area with my kit, I surveyed a different kind of Sherman far removed from the tidy jobs at Bovington; these parked-up in a snug wood had a well used and organised look: they wore camouflage netting with their backs loaded with boxes and other kit, and all had track plates welded round the turret sides as an extra protection against bazookas. In a more domestic contrast to all the hardware, were several pairs of underpants draped to dry over a gun barrel, a detail that made me wonder fleetingly whether they related in any way to the regiment's recent combat reputation. A couple of crewmen were busy shoving a long cleaning rod up and down their clothes-line gun barrel, and from the open turret came the hum of a radio switched on to listening net. Beyond its sharp edges the scene appeared to be comfortably organised, and I relaxed a bit.

The business of joining a crew didn't take too long either; everyone made me welcome, but looked speculatively at me — they'd been at it for a while and here was I, fresh from England and probably not knowing my arse from my elbow — but at least they were sensitive enough to take their time before telling me that the crew member I was replacing had inadvertently stepped on a mine. What must have been even more worrying for them was the fact I was to take over the turret gun; they'd have been more worried still had they known that my main training had focused on radio operation and loading — though in fact, my gunnery was good, gun sights being very accurate if properly adjusted, and up to then I'd hit everything I aimed at, despite that blistered hand on my final tests.

For a few days as we shook down, they must have worried about me — but then seemed to relax. Under the direction of Brem our tank commander (whose easy matter-of-fact presence was, for me, enhanced by a nicotine stained moustache which appeared to serve as a general-purpose filter), fire orders over the intercom were cool, measured and spot-on accurate; thanks to him it didn't take long for me to distinguish arse from elbow as far as real world gunnery was concerned. His calm was a big influence in settling a novice — there's a lot of difference between shooting at a mock-up target on the ranges at Lulworth, and getting your sights on a

149

tank with crosses on its side — especially your first one. That was my main hurdle really. For years, the enemy had been shown by pictures and films, something recorded and at a safe distance — now dreadfully, he was there in the flesh, or steel, only a killing distance away, and a reciprocated killing distance at that. Awareness froze me: I felt a tight band of fear clamp round my chest and I couldn't breathe. "I can't handle this" — it was a black moment of panic — then mercifully training kicked in, and I was functioning again. It happened that first time — a big step from one reality to something quite different — a step everybody I knew had taken at one time or another.

As a teacher Brem was a natural. There are basic rules to the business of fighting enemy tanks, the most important of which is to see him first — if you didn't he'd probably blow you away — an easily assimilated concept: "I do the seeing", he remarked warming to the lesson, "you do the hitting in the right place: the right place is not the front or side armour, especially on Tigers. The right place — if he doesn't show you his arse," he went on, "is where turret and hull meet — an armour-piercing shot popped in there — even if it doesn't penetrate, will most likely jam the turret, and a jammed turret can't traverse and lay its gun. Bingo! At which point we sneak round the back and shoot him up what he didn't show you in the first place, so he won't bother us any more. Do that a time or two" he went on, "and I shall get a medal while you'll still be alive enough to brew the tea. That's the theory, anyway."

It was soon obvious to me that the German army, man for man, was as good at soldiering as we were, if not better — and equally obvious was the fact that their ordnance be it tank or gun, with few exceptions were certainly superior. Ideas like that once instilled leave a kind of fatalistic general acceptance, with a particular resonance regarding Tiger tanks with their murderous 88mm guns, and the Panther with its lesser but still very effective 75mm armament. The ubiquitous Mark 4 Panzerkampfwagen, their Sherman equivalent, we felt better able to cope with — it was much more in our league.

They hadn't told us at Bovington that Sherman tanks were known as Ronson Lighters, supposedly by our enemies as well — and it didn't take long to find out why. In many ways though, it wasn't a bad tank: more crew-friendly in terms of space and equipment than others; it was fitted with a power traverse motor to rotate the turret fast, and ventilation to clear cordite smoke worked well, details like that make a big difference. Anyway, we'd been told often enough that an inferior tank efficiently crewed, had a better than even chance against a superior one poorly handled — machinery is just machinery, they said, its training and brains that count — in other words chaps, don't blame your tools. Quite. At full strength, which wasn't often, there were five tank troops to a squadron, three tanks to a troop, of which two were short-gun diesel-engine Shermans, the third being the British converted petrol engine Firefly Sherman with its high-velocity gun firing

151

tungsten-tipped shot which could dent even a Tiger tank.

An operational day, like a bank holiday at the seaside, often produced unexpected twists and turns and could last longer than one thought possible — sometimes with little to show for it except exhaustion and a mouth that approximated to the floor of the proverbial parrot cage. In your seat maybe for twelve hours at a time, major bodily functions could have been an issue since tanks don't run to lavatories, but somehow our systems seemed to adapt. Need for a pee was easy to accommodate, an empty shell case (not a hot one) was passed round then jettisoned over the side; the extra long shell case on the Firefly was particularly popular being more capacious and could contain pretty well the whole offerings of its four man crew.

At the end of each operational day, if time allowed, your tank had to be refuelled, topped up with ammunition, and its guns, engine and suspension units serviced; it seemed to me the suspension bogeys and idlers had a million grease nipples, each requiring the requisite number of grease-gun strokes — but it was crucial work, anything seizing-up down there and we weren't going anywhere. Replacement of ammunition was a particularly tedious job especially in the dark; for a start there was a lot to carry, and each shell for the main gun had to be in mint condition. Given the smallest dent in the brass casing, it was almost certain to jam in the breech — a rotten job to sort out, not only in having to get out of the tank in unhealthy conditions, but also involved shoving a rod up the barrel to dislodge the round — OK if it was a jammed armour-piercing one, dodgy if it happened to be the explosive kind.

Supply and maintenance was work often carried out when it was dark and wet; sometimes the "soft" echelons who supplied us couldn't get all that near to where we were leaguered, so a crew would have to hump ammunition and more than a 100gals of fuel (about a day's consumption) in 4½gal jerricans, maybe half a mile across a field or two; if the war had gone on much longer, we'd all have had arms as long and muscled as a gorilla's. The diesel fuel, "Derv" as it's called, was sulphurous with a sort of gone off egg resonance that had an uncanny ability of getting just about everywhere — and I mean everywhere, doing little to spice up a spoonful of cold pudding if it was that sort of day. If you've filled up your car with diesel recently and forgotten to use the plastic gloves supplied, multiply the smell on your fingers by a factor of ten and you'll have some idea of its qualities as an appetiser.

Nevertheless, we ate well from our compo rations, boxes containing goodies such as treacle puddings, chocolate and cigarettes, as well as more basic rations; you had to like your tea with milk powder and sugar added, because it didn't come any other way. There was also the ubiquitous Donald Cook's Delicious Stewed Steak [sic] in its white tin with blue lettering. Donald must have had a pretty good war all tins considered, since I never opened a compo box without finding his offerings waiting for me. "That's the way to do it", as Punch would have remarked, produce something that armies need to eat, shoot or wear, and you're made. But I fear that Donald wasn't loved: "Cook Donald" or "Sod Donald" were common among the more polite mantras when opening his distinctive tins. In fairness, what he gave us was pretty good, especially if there was time enough to forage about and make up a stew with vegetables or whatever; it was less appetising though if you had to feed on the hoof, digging into a tin with its head of white congealed fat. If we had any time in one place, we'd live off the land as much as we could as items like poultry were particularly sought after, and we carried a "borrowed" .22 rifle for anything that could run faster than us.

After dark if we hadn't drawn the short straw of guard duty, we'd snug up inside the tank, hang berets over the periscopes to stop any light escaping and read our mail if any had come up with the rations. Sometimes Joe our operator would switch the radio off listening net, and hunt for American or British Forces Network stations around the airwaves — not all that easy as the radio didn't work well at night, especially in wooded country. Sometimes though, he scored a bull and we'd get a snatch of Glenn Miller, smooth and syrupy — antithesis to the day's proceedings; best of all for me, was a moment or two of Johnny Mercer or Hoagy Carmichael, unmistakeable with their quirky songs: *You gotta accentuate the positive, eliminate the negative, latch on to the affirmative and don't mess with Mr In Between* (good advice, that!). You don't get to hear Hoagy much these days, but I've only to recognise a snatch from that unmistakeable voice and I'm back over sixty something years in a flash. Miller and Hoagy were like balm to a burn.

Being one of the regiments in the 8th Armoured Brigade — one of the two special Monty's Marauder brigades — meant we were often used as a kind of troubleshooting unit, which involved action with a variety of French, Polish and Canadian outfits, as well as more homely sounding infantry regiments such as the Lincolnshires — distinguished if I remember right, by their differently shaped helmets. We worked a bit with American airborne units and sometimes enjoyed a change of rations, swapping items of ours for their K-Rations; we smoked their Camel cigarettes too, amused at the effect of our lethal Capstan Full Strength on their lungs. I always thought the taste of those Camels was most appropriate to the name. I'm happy to report that we had no problems with "friendly fire" from the Yankee regiments we supported — evidently the grandfathers (great grandfathers?) of today's American army were a lot better disciplined and not all that surprising when you compare the campaigns.

CHAPTER
TWENTY-THREE

From Somewhere up Front

The routine for our day activities usually started well before first light, whenever that happened to be. Blearily I'd attempt a shave in cold water — anything hot was reserved for a brew up of tea, after which it was a case of scratching around for something to eat though the day's prospect never did much for anybody's appetite. Then you'd fill time by checking that everything still worked, while waiting for tank commanders to come back from Orders Groups with details of the day's activities — their expressions usually a good pointer to what was expected of us.

Waiting on the start line was always fraught, a strange time of apprehension mixed with an occasional awareness of how lovely things seem when the world shapes up again after the night. Once I heard a cockerel tune up from somewhere far beyond the German positions. Chanticleer was busy with preoccupations far more absorbing than fighting a war, his voice coming in loud and clear over the grumble of our warming up engines: it was a moment seeming both incongruous and wonderful in a lifting mist that made the ground ahead seem, briefly, almost beautiful. Those of us who had the ears to hear him, wished him well — who knows, he might have been a talisman for a safer day.

After the morning's preliminaries, the most usual pattern, except for dealing with counter attacks, was German army defending and us attacking, a case of making the first move — much the worse of two evils. It's a good deal more relaxing to be sitting hull down in a chosen position with the ground in front previously ranged, and wait with a mug of tea and a compo chocolate bar for an obliging target to turn up — but you don't gain ground and lose wars less badly than your opponents like that. What you do when you move from start line is to leave relatively safe cover in a sort of mini "over the top" — take or fail to take the chosen objective — this sometimes for days at a time in the same murderous pantomime that painfully moves little flags on the newspapers' maps in directions that were likely to help digestion, as well as keep Montgomery and Eisenhower happy.

Enemy counter attacks were unpredictable and often presaged by a sudden concentration of incoming fire designed to keep our heads down — especially the infantry's; sometimes it would be an attempt to retake a village or some useful observation point like a church tower. Sometimes over the racket, you'd hear the ominous sound of tank engines and the clatter of tracks — and know that certainly their infantry would be close behind. With our Browning machine guns loaded up, and the main gun's breechblock open ready to receive the round most urgently needed — armour piercing or explosive — there was the waiting through long tripwire seconds, eyes straining for that first movement, running figures might appear, you already had the range — so you set the sights, aiming off a fraction to allow for what are likely to be their last steps.

Some blessed times nothing happened, as if they'd decided it wasn't such a good idea after all; more often though they put down smoke shells as a preliminary, which was bad news because concentrated smoke allows things to get too close. In reduced visibility a fire order can come late and doesn't always get you on target straight away, which isn't what you want when it's probable your opposite number is doing the same thing — but looking for you.

In the end of course, what was going to happen, happened, but as I've mentioned, it was at least a reversal of our usual role and rather more comfortable to be ready and waiting in a chosen position. If things went well we'd see them first and clobber them until they backed off, and then our position would be further consolidated by whichever infantry we were supporting. At other times if we'd pushed too far, or found ourselves too exposed we'd do the backing off, then call in supporting fire from mobile artillery, which was usually not far off. Any engagement large or small had (still has no doubt) the same mix of ingredients: fear, noise, vile acrid smells and poor visibility caused by smoke from various origins — each contributing to any battle's fundamental element — that of confusion.

158

What you did was to fight your own corner and hope for the best.

Occasionally a situation required a foot reconnaissance when something more discreet than a blundering tank was needed to check out what might be waiting for us around a corner. I remember feeling particularly naked on my first excursion, missing the relative safety of my turret — but old habits die hard, and Moor Park ferreting with its hostile gamekeepers came to the rescue. Fundamentally nothing was different and you used the cover whatever it was, kept quiet and your head down. If you've ever learned the lessons of the rightness and wrongness of things — like a hedge unaccountably too dense, or a shadow in a place it hadn't been a moment before, it'll always be a part of you. I'm sure it's something in our gene bank that goes back thousands of years and now has become dormant with civilisation yet it's still there. The object of a foot recce wasn't primarily to make contact, it was just to have a shufti, as the army expressed it, to find out what was where; if things got heavy you backed off, which was right up my street. Usually I'd feel a strong sense of *déjà vu* on these expeditions, available cover being much the same as that which Tom and I had used in Shropshire, and I'd have the memory of Oscar at the back of my mind at such times — he was reassuring mental company. As I said, it was the same game really — but with the stakes somewhat higher.

Ground support operations as distinct from armoured thrusts — what we called "swanning" on roads — had another dimension; any tank has to be a mobile compromise: designers have somehow to incorporate engine power, solid armour and an effective main gun — and all these involve weight. Put thirty tons of Sherman on a soggy field and it sinks with the alacrity of a happy hippo diving into its wallow — you're then in dead trouble, particularly if your opposite numbers have previously ranged the ground. At best, extrication is time-consuming, and your only friends are your towrope (two if you've managed to steal a spare), and somebody close by, who isn't stuck and able to pull you out.

Certainly ground conditions would have been a major consideration for those planning an open-country attack involving armour and infantry, which is where the fast-moving reconnaissance units in light armour came into their own — but it's easy to miss the wet bits you haven't actually driven over. Happily, the German tank commanders would have had the same worries as us since their Tigers weighed sixty tons or so and Panthers over forty, which would have made their crews much more wary about stepping off the road: certainly this must have been an exceedingly dangerous limiting factor at times. The comforting presence of armour 6-8ins thick came at a price.

When weight worries weren't bugging them, German tank commanders were adept at the business of concealment, an essential element in defensive fighting. One ploy we came across was to back up into a house or barn with big doorways — they'd make them bigger when necessary — then cover up their protruding gun barrel with a camouflage net and await developments.

On one occasion we had been warned of such a lurking Tiger by observant infantry; a foot recce showed us a gun draped with unconvincing bits and pieces sticking out of a barn door trying to look like farm equipment; we backed off, and by a circuitous route got round behind the barn and its lurking occupant. The barn was one with big openings at the back and front, with the tank silhouetted against the daylight outside; its crew must have heard us coming, but a very solid vertical beam holding up the barn roof, prevented its gunner from traversing the heart-stopping length of his 88 anywhere near us — and thus became the much sought after sitting duck. A couple of armour-piercing shots into his back end from a cheeky range of a 100yds or so was all that was needed, and he brewed up straight away — unfortunately both barn and farmhouse caught fire as well. The moral, I suppose, is that sometimes you can be really clever and still not see an obvious downside — at any rate it was a mistake that crew weren't going to make twice. Thus the industrial process of war: machine against machine, operated by boys playing men's games, except they weren't games, and the finality of death was real.

There was on one occasion a lighter moment at start-line time. One morning just as the sun was rising (as goes the song), Obie Walker our hull gunner was seriously absent: big panic in the form of the Squadron Sergeant Major storming up at the double — a most unusual sight.

"What's this, desertion in the face of the enemy? My God! Whole brigade's stopped in its tracks (not meant

161

as a joke I think) Regiment's reputation at stake." all that along with many other anguished fragments in similar vein. For a few moments depressed spirits rise. "Can't go in with incomplete crew can we?" It doesn't take much to raise hopes but it isn't to be. Obie, not hurrying overmuch, appears from a discreet clump of bushes adjusting his trousers.

"Where the f**k have you been?"

"Having a s**t, sir."

"You know what you've done? You've held up the whole bloody brigade — probably the whole army as well. Good mind to put you on a charge!"

"Gotta have a s**t, sir — when you gotta go you . . ."

"Shuddup!" It's very unusual for the SSM to be out of breath or lost for words, and he can't waste time doing what he'd like to do which is to throttle Obie there and then, there's a whole war at stake.

"I'll be watching you like a hawk, Walker, one more wrong move and I'll hang you up by your goolies, you hear me? Get back to your crew." And thus entertained, squadron, brigade and probably the whole British Second Army, moves on into history.

At more serious moments, when flying conditions allowed, we had the very great advantage of being able to call up supporting air strikes when encountering something too tough to cope with ourselves. Brigade would get back to RAF forward strike squadrons with accurate map references, then we'd hang about with large fluorescent markers stretched out over the back of the tank — hopefully there to be spotted good and early as being us by the pilot when he arrived. Within twenty minutes or so, a rocket-carrying Typhoon or Tempest (I can't remember which), would appear at very low level, make a pass, guided by our tracer fired at the target sitting maybe 3-400yds distant, then turn into another run and let fly with its rockets. Those missiles fired from pretty near zero-zero feet were deadly, making a shambles of the toughest target — often dumping a turret yards away from the smoking heap of what was left. It was great shooting, and those pilots must have possessed hawks' eyes — but it was close stuff for us — with absolutely no room for mistakes. More often than not, my eyes were shut and my fingers crossed, you can't order luck, but you're certainly grateful when she turns up.

One day our suspension and tracks were damaged by a direct hit which exploded rather than penetrated; where possible you sorted out such damage yourself, an uncomfortable process with the probability of more incoming fire arriving from where the first came from. While investigating the damage we found what was left of an infantryman who must have been walking beside us: he was lying close by with his head split like a walnut and with other parts of him distributed among the twisted remains of the track plates and bogeys of our suspension. As I said, repairs to that sort of damage were something we practised often at Bovington and had continued elsewhere, but this was of a different magnitude, upsetting us all. Dirt was an ongoing factor in our lives, but sometimes we felt more than dirty.

A chance for a serious clean up soon became a pressing matter, but would have to wait until we had been relieved by another regiment and had pulled back to a rest area; it doesn't take long for one's body to become disgusting, and it was wonderful to wallow in a makeshift bath or have a hot shower and put on new underclothes — our used ones were usually burned. Occasionally the pioneers, who imaginatively built the facilities from not very much, got it wrong and I remember showers being rigged up in a barn with an earthen floor — but I didn't care, most of me was clean.

CHAPTER
TWENTY-FOUR

Brussels Without Sprouts

Occasionally pulling back to a rest area also meant a forty-eight-hour trip to civilisation; after Brussels was taken, this was the place if distance wasn't a factor. We'd sheet up the tanks, draw quite a lot of back pay, collect best uniform from the quartermaster, then truck it to the rest centre at Louvain just outside Brussels — there to eat and sleep a lot before hitting town to see what was what. Short leaves like that were great — while they lasted, but forty-eight hours of contrast made the going back a gloomy affair. Being knackered after too much of everything, as well as being broke and dispirited at the prospect of the mixture as before, made return journeys to wherever it was, a moody affair.

Brussels never had the looks or cachet of Paris, but it adapted to changing circumstance pretty quickly. Scarcely had the last panzers left the outskirts before the business ladies had successfully adapted to a new regime. When several armies of like-minded people fresh from the sharp-edge areas of a war converge on a city, it's not surprising that business is likely to be good.

Naturally the women in our lives were to be as transient as ourselves as we pushed by fits and starts across north-west Europe; in contrast to soldiers in the First World War who were stuck in a trench in one place for most of the time, we didn't stay for long anywhere. But when I think of women, I think particularly of Holland and a town called Hengelo or maybe it was Enschede, not that it matters. I was much blessed in Holland entirely because everybody thought I looked just like their Prince Bernhardt. He was a revered member of the Dutch Royal Family and, wonderfully, many of Bernhardt's fine qualities were attributed to "Gerry Bernhardt" who looked so very, very like him — and so must be a lad of good morals and intent (this the parents' view), which was most flattering.

But in a world apart was Anna who had come from the south of Holland and wasn't blonde and pink — who arrived like a shooting star into my life. She showed me another dimension, all very callow and Hollywood "B" movie stuff I suppose, but it was new and I thought it was love, something far removed from what I hoped I'd begun to get the hang of up to then. Perhaps we somehow struck a magic spark briefly lighting up our lives that touched only for a day or two. Never when it came could a dawn promise so little when we moved on, as we always did. I never saw her again.

However, women weren't the only preoccupation, because in those days there wasn't time or space in which to dwell on what you thought you'd lost — or found. Holland was the first country where, very occasionally, there were opportunities of staying a few days with a family, our tanks parked incongruously outside their houses like cars are today: it was an experience that offered other insights. The Dutch had gone really short of food before we arrived (remember the RAF food drops agreed with the Germans in those last weeks?), so we were doubly welcome. I remember opening a compo pack in a kitchen (our stores echelon were aware of the situation and often had "spare" rations if we asked nicely), with the family standing round gawping, but with Mum in tears — all they'd had for months were potatoes. It was salutary for us, since most of the time we had been at one remove from civilians except on occasions when it was safe enough to give us a welcome on entering a town, but those we measured in thousands not families. It was good to see Mum happy, though still bothered by the fact she thought us to be so young: she'd look at us and shake her head while Dad, who spoke good English, would translate. But by then we weren't all that young any more.

Of all the towns and countries we went through, it was across the Dutch border where people were collectively the most enthusiastic, or maybe just more inventive. As we rolled into town with the Germans rolling out (we hoped) on the other side, windows would open and the red, white and blue or orange flags (or both) would come fluttering out, and the streets would suddenly be filled with colour and people. Stop for a moment and your tank would disappear under cheering multitudes oblivious of possible rearguard snipers, our loaded guns — or our increasingly inaudible warnings. If there's any glamour at all in fighting a campaign, I suppose it's in moments like those — allied tanks and uniforms after years of occupation must have been a wonderful sight for them, and to us it was good to be feeling something other than just tired and dirty.

If the campaign was a grind for us, it must have been a lot harder for our opposite numbers who had virtually no air support, dwindling supplies of everything vital like fuel and ammunition, and probably with few rest centres either — all that in a fight against opponents who apparently had unlimited supplies of everything. There's a story, probably apocryphal, of a German battery commander complaining bitterly that he'd run out of ammunition before the enemy had run out of tanks. We had a muted respect for the Wehrmacht — as long as they weren't associating with SS units, and probably they had the same feeling for us — English dirt and exhaustion being much the same as anybody else's. And as the war drew to its close, they had the added pressure of knowing they were fighting for their homeland: for us it was an away match — and that was a very different matter.

Sometimes though, the "them and us" factor became a bit more personal. I remember coming across a solitary grave in a space of open ground fringed by a forest splintered by shellfire. The grave was freshly dug and tidy, with an improvised cross held together with

168

string; on the cross was placed a German helmet with a gash in its side you could've put your fist through. It seemed such a lonely place. Alive, you spend most of your time among people — at home, school, army, whatever, that's pretty well the way of what might have been a life lived in parallel with yours — until you wind-up in a shallow grave without most of your head, with little around you except ruined trees and a passing stranger who had been your enemy. Moments like that make you shockingly aware of your own vulnerability.

The trouble is that there are no limits to warfare — anything goes, from the perceived outline of a soldier (origin unknown), flattened to one dimension in the middle of a road by armoured units who had just gone over him regardless, to the sight of bewildered refugees loaded with what little they still possessed, being harried out of the way. Once an emaciated horse bolted and tipped its cart, occupants and everything else, down a steep embankment. Nobody stopped. Afterwards, usually long afterwards, you wonder beyond the physicality of it all, think about our lemming-like willingness to act beyond the reasonable; it's at that point I suppose, where expediency supplants conscience. There's an army song that repetitively choruses: "We're here because we're here because we're here." One might add: "We do because we do because we do."

There's another implicit element that makes its presence felt in combat conditions — the hate factor. There are several manifestations of this: many might quote the malevolent presence of snipers — never realised until too late — the killers who took such toll

169

of tank commanders not allowed to depend on their periscopes. But I've always thought that booby traps come pretty high up the list of these variations. Booby traps were — and doubtless still are — an ever-present threat when following up a retreating enemy; out of the tank we walked on eggs, touched as little as possible when investigating anything abandoned. German S-mines — those devastating little canisters that jump 3ft in the air before exploding, were the principal danger: they eviscerated as well as killed and might be activated anywhere (probably much the same in their effect as the cluster bombs that were dropped by the Americans and RAF near villages in Iraq not long ago).

In a house we'd planned to sleep in, we heard the squeaky miaowing of a kitten shut in a cupboard; wise by then, we checked it out with great care and found the tell-tale wiring and trigger (often booby trapped as well) that would have activated the explosive when the cupboard door was opened. Such action doesn't slow down advances or prevent objectives being taken, and individuals who might have died rescuing a kitten would be just a couple more casualties, to be replaced with a metaphorical shrug — *c'est la guerre* — although in the heads of SS units, the usual perpetrators, such an act would most likely have represented rather more than that. In the event I've described, we left chapter and verse written on the door for the sappers, and slept somewhere else.

Sometimes the unpredictable was more abstract. Occasionally if conditions were warm and dry enough, I'd sleep out under the tank to stretch my legs, which had been coiled under my seat all day. One such night I couldn't sleep: it was quiet, no gunfire, no movement, but there was an odd persistent sound seeming to be everywhere and yet nowhere. I would liken it to a tenor church bell long since struck, but with its resonance still not entirely dead. A look at a map next morning told us we had leaguered near an old battlefield. I wondered if that sound was always there at night, whether cataclysmic events go on echoing in other dimensions — sometimes to leak into ours.

Experience tells me that the worst moments of involvement in a campaign are nearly always the quiet ones when imagination has time to take over. Often at night when things have slowed down, individual sounds assume greater significance than they would in daylight — the not-so-distant racket of enemy armour moving around for example; for us, such sounds by day were a commonplace scenario, but night added unreasonable but real dimensions of apprehension. When there's nothing to do there's time to think, personal ogres to confront, and even proximity with others doing the same as you, counts for little.

Fatigue was a fact of life you got used to and could handle given a few hours of rest — though sometimes when things had gone on longer than usual, you just dropped into a black hole of sleep pretty well wherever you happened to be when there was a bit of time. Provision in the form of Benzedrine was made for operations that went on maybe for days and nights: it kept you awake — but you had a huge let down when the effects wore off, and nobody liked using the stuff because of that.

Battle fatigue so-called — a very different beast that had only begun to be understood in Second World War — was a factor I only saw once in my unit. One morning at start-up time, one of the drivers got into his tank as usual, settled in his seat — then seemed to freeze, staring unblinkingly in front of him — a kind of catatonic state I suppose. His brain had just seized up and couldn't take another day of the mixture as before, which was too much stress for too long. In the end, and with some difficulty, he was extricated from the tank and taken off to a field station — thence, I suppose, to hospital — and we didn't see the poor guy again. It's horrific to think that he would probably have been shot for cowardice had it happened in the First World War.

Recollection haunts like a ghost. There was the old man on the wrong side of the Dutch border who walked in the rain across an open field towards us — in his cupped hands he was holding a few eggs: he came so close he was almost looking down the barrels of our guns, which had followed his every step. He stood there offering what he had but was waved brusquely away. He was German, a time-scarred farmer trying to save his farm by giving what little he had. Later, you think about how desperate you have to be to walk painfully out under enemy guns — to offer, and then be rejected by a gesture and curt "*Raus!*" End of story, except it wasn't. I wondered then how he felt — have been wondering ever since.

One morning I was in the turret sorting out the main gun of a replacement tank, our previous vehicle having taken what was probably an 88mm shot through its engine a few days earlier, the shot striking us with the force of a lightning bolt (I've a fair idea of how the unfortunate blasted oak feels on impact). Rupturing the fuel tanks, impact and ignition were simultaneous, thus provoking the famous Ronson Factor — a tall pillar of oily smoke and a fire from which you'd never pull a chestnut. We bailed out (omitting to follow the idiot procedures as laid down by Bovington Standing Orders) fast enough to qualify for scalded cat status, though scorched cat might be more appropriate.

American economic power was a significant reason why Germany lost the war, its manufacturing base could produce everything needed in large quantities; one of these commodities was the Sherman tank, which could be produced from prefabricated parts in thirty minutes at the factory — so plenty of replacements were available when needed. As a Sherman-equipped regiment — as were most RAC tank regiments — the spin off for crews was that there was little respite between losing one tank, for whatever reason, and being given another. This was great for generals who wanted to keep their little flags moving — but maybe not so great for the surviving crews who wouldn't have minded a few days off.

I expect I was mulling over all that while I worked to persuade a factory-fresh gun and its sights to focus on the same place at the same time, when somebody clambered up outside and poked his head in through the cupola hatch "How's it going, young man?" a voice enquired. It was Brigadier Horrocks who was well known for riding around in a Cromwell tank (faster than a Sherman) so he could keep a personal eye on what was going on outside headquarters — and was likely to turn up anywhere at any time. I was fed up enough not to be fazed by his sudden appearance in my turret and we had a good conversation, talking shop about tanks and related matters: his questions were relevant and he appeared to show genuine interest as he listened to my answers.

I realised then that this was leadership at its best, instilling a rare personal touch to those near the bottom of the pile — and because of that, getting the best from them. Horrocks was a popular figure in our brigade and earlier had been near enough to the proverbial cutting edge to pick up a wound — not all that common among senior officers. But I realised also that underneath the humane laid-back exterior, he was still a professional soldier doing the thing that fulfilled ambition and paid his salary — a profession in which human lives were just one more expendable resource among many. And I had an illuminating think about that.

Long after the war, I watched General Brian Horrocks, as he had then become, present a television programme on the conduct of the Overlord Campaign; in front of the cameras he was as relaxed as he'd been in my tank. With blackboard and maps he took us through the battles, the problems, successes and setbacks, rather in the manner of an expert describing a complex surgical procedure; as I watched his little flags move forward, I wondered how many white crosses were being left behind — and speculated on how, both as general and man, he coped with the reality of that.

Perhaps the most unexpected event that had come about in those unsettled days was the fact that Stanley and I met up in some gloomy part of Holland, if I remember correctly. By extraordinary chance in all the organised chaos of a campaign, our regiments briefly coincided. Aware of that and with an hour to spare, we hunted each other down in that particular bit of jungle — and met up as if it had been previously arranged. I took Stan back to where we were parked and brewed up mugs of compo tea. But despite the pleasure of seeing each other again, we found conversation strangely inhibited: to me it was a surreal experience, a collision of what as children we had represented to each other — with an uneasy reality and all it implied — and with weaponry that wasn't measured in catapults any more. Years later we talked about that hour we spent together in some forgotten place — our reactions, it seemed, had been much the same and had created a crack in the carapace, unsettling us both. And soon after that, my mood was not lightened by the news that my friend Miles had been killed a few days earlier in action with another squadron.

CHAPTER
TWENTY-FIVE

Rhine Jump and a Bit Further On

Water, except that which had bounced our landing craft uncomfortably about off the end of Southend Pier on our way to war, and the nasty metallic-tasting stuff we carried with us in jerricans, had played little part in our progress eastwards. Such water obstacles as we'd encountered, either miraculously had bridges that hadn't been destroyed or were crossed by pontoons — the building of which was something else the engineers were brilliant at achieving. But all that changed in March 1945 when we eventually got to the Rhine, a major obstacle which had to be crossed; it was a requirement made tricky by the fact that it was wide, very fast flowing — and the bridges in our sector had been blown up by inconsiderate rearguards. For this operation we were held in reserve to be rafted over the river when the area was secured. Rafted? Certainly, they said — it's dead easy, it floats and you just sit on it and it's all done for you. Well — if you say so, but rafts to me were flat things you dived off a few comfortable yards from your beach in summer, and were certainly no place for a tank.

There was the niggling uncertainty of this form of transport worrying us, when earlier we moved out of what was left of the Rhineland town of Goch where we'd holed up for a week or so, travelling past a naked female shop window dummy strategically sited beside the road with a notice saying "Goodbye Temptation" hung around her neck. Thus fortified, we arrived on the west bank of the river in time for the spectacle of a sky full of Dakotas disgorging their loads of Paras onto the far side of the Rhine; it was a large drop from not very high, but they seemed to float down so slowly in those vulnerable seconds before reaching the ground, that I think we all held our breath for them, I know I did. In the end it seemed a successful drop with little opposition, and as far as we could tell, nobody finished up by taking an unwelcome swim. I remember thinking that if I had to fight a war, I would much prefer to do it in the relative safety of a tank, and at least there was no obligation to jump out of aeroplanes — then have to do the rest on foot.

After the entertainment it got to be our turn. When we arrived at the crossing point it was becoming dark, the river as far as we could see looked about ten miles wide, and the bank against which a number of frail-looking floating contraptions sucked and burped, appeared as near sheer as made little difference — and muddy. What seemed clear was the ugly fact that once over the top of that bank there was no going back. We had been issued with life jackets, which nobody forgot

177

to put on, and at the appropriate time with some resignation, we prepared ourselves for the possibility of a long swim.

Taking a deep breath, several deep breaths, we metaphorically held our noses and drove over the edge to our allocated transport. Somehow Smith, our driver, managed the bank and pussy footed us onto a raft that sucked and burped even more ferociously while it accepted our very laden weight. This engineers' brainchild was guided between cables attached to each bank and winched across the river by more cables fixed fore and aft for return journeys. We worried about such things as their tensile strength and hoped fervently that they would hold together long enough to get us across. At that point we didn't care a straw what was waiting for us in the tracer-perforated darkness ahead — just get us there!

Several oceans' worth of very cold water in a hurry to swamp the North Sea greedily sucked and gobbled at us as we slowly creaked and wallowed across that gigantic Styx, nobody wanted to stay inside the tank — even incoming fire was preferable as we huddled unhappily as far from water as we could get. After several lifetimes we were close enough to note the approaching bank was as steep as the other, while Smith who couldn't swim thoughtfully sucked his teeth — at least we had gravity with us when embarking, but this bank was seriously uphill. However, with engine bellowing, tracks spewing huge clods of mud, he got us up and over. We loved him for it.

After the crossing there were still a few weeks of the campaign left, with things to do and places to visit; it was clear up stuff mostly, but with a few bitter engagements with rearguards still to play out. Our first mission was to head for the coast and neutralise any flying-bomb launching sites in the area, which wasn't much of a problem since most had been abandoned. It was interesting to see how many of these missiles had failed to get off their launching ramps, the areas around being thickly littered with craters and bits, like abandoned junkyards. What proportion of the total launches these failures represented we had no clue, but it must have been considerable and should have been at least something of a plus as far as potential targets had been concerned.

All that being so easy meant it wasn't going to last — and before long we found ourselves joining the rest of 30 Corps in the advance again. Around 21 April (the date of my wedding day six years later), we were given the job of attacking and securing the east side of Bremen, an action that took us slowly through the suburbs in daylight. At the beginning of the day we had heard the city's air raid sirens in full cry — to my ear they sounded exactly the same as ours at home and I wished my parents could have heard them; it might have given them a buzz. Street fighting is always particularly unpleasant, everything is too close — making the likelihood of being hit by a bazooka or finding a waiting panzer holed up somewhere unexpected even more real — and the unexpected had a habit of lurking round every corner. However, the

179

presence of infantry — if I remember right we had the Somersets with us — made a big difference. The attack continued after nightfall which was more bad news, but by then we had reached the city centre.

What followed is stamped vividly in my memory because it was the first time I'd done big-city fighting at night supported by flame-throwing Churchill tanks, which gushed and snorted fire like bad-tempered dragons. Actually there wasn't much left to do, our main problem was getting entangled with overhanging tram wires — but it seemed to me as if it all had been carefully staged: a theatre of the damned, the infantry with their fixed bayonets silhouetted against the great spurts of fire licking into the dark shadowed buildings, sometimes to flush out potential snipers. Between the sounding boards of house and street lay the heavy stink of flamethrower fuel, cordite, s**t and fear — an apocalyptic scene that the painter Goya might have relished. I mention all that, not because it was a hard action — it wasn't, but because of its amazingly atmospheric effect. There's much I've forgotten about those times, but I'll never forget that night.

After Bremen our activities slowed up somewhat, and as far as the world's press was concerned it seemed the war was over — fait accompli and all that. One day we had a visit from a war correspondent, an American, looking the business in combat fatigues with a big six-shooter on his hip. He climbed out of his Jeep with the white-circled star on its sides, daringly accepted a Capstan Full Strength, and regaled us with General Patton's big advances which, he said, had already done for the opposition down south — unspoken criticism, I'd guess, of our less dramatic progress in the north.

"Forty miles a day? Zat's motorin' — not fightin'" commented Pancho, our Columbian mercenary who'd been driving tanks since the days of Wadi Zem-Zem in North Africa, "bloody 'ell we got real panzers up 'ere — big buggers too." (Pancho's English was as colloquial as anybody's.) Later we watched our visitor depart in a flurry of dust. "Bloody 'Ollywood" observed Pancho with contempt, "'e know f**k all about ennyzing," and laughed. He'd used up most of his nine lives by then, but still had the wonderful knack of making everybody feel good, as usual he was on form.

Theoretically we were in pursuit of remaining enemy forces, I say theoretically because we didn't find many troops to pursue — also progress suddenly became more difficult. To slow down our movements, German units were sowing the roads with 500lb bombs or sea-mines — those enormous round things with knobs on that sink battleships. One afternoon later in April, we were doing a probe when the world blew up in front of us — a great red ball flew overhead like a newly minted meteor in a graceful parabola, to disappear behind a line of trees half a mile away. Who had departed this life with such panache we never discovered, since there was nothing left except a very large smoking crater in the road. We knew there were none of our forces ahead of us, so the assumption was that some unfortunate rearguard had made a serious mistake — which was particularly lucky for us as we

181

were leading tank that day. After that no stone — no inch of road, so to speak, was left unstudied.

There was another problem to contend with — an old enemy with a new and unpleasant twist. In those last weeks of war the Hitler Youth was brought in to try to delay the inevitable. These lads issued with uniforms and helmets that looked a size too big for them, were aged around thirteen or fourteen — sometimes much younger — and had been drafted in from school, hastily trained to fire Panzerfausts (bazooka-type anti-tank weapons), and were soon operating with retreating regular Wehrmacht units. Schoolboys they might have been — extremely dangerous they certainly were. The Panzerfausts was a weapon best used from close range and — as always — roads with hedges or ditches were a particular hazard to us. Usually operating singly, a small boy camouflaged and hiding with his panzerfaust was not easily spotted, with the result that many tanks were knocked out by them. Observation like timing was all, and tank commanders kept an even greater supply of grenades handy for when one of these lads was spotted too close to be dealt with by our guns — and that was a lot too close. Hitler spared nobody.

It's quite strange I suppose, that you can spend months fighting your enemy without speaking to one personally; sometimes you shouted at prisoners, waved them back to where they could be picked up by infantry, but *"Raus! Schnell!"* and other bits of fractured German are hardly conversation. One day when things had quietened down, Joe and I had gone for a foot reconnaissance to see what problems lay ahead; we were slinking along a grassy track beside some woods, when we spotted a solitary German soldier apparently tinkering with the engine of a staff car. He hadn't seen us, so we did our Red Indian approach thing with Sten guns cocked. Startled, he straightened up from what he'd been working on with his hands shooting skywards. "*Scheisse!*" he exclaimed — then collecting himself, he looked at us and nodded toward the track we'd just walked along. "*Minen*" he said, "many, many!" Joe and I looked at each other and reached for our cigarettes. We'd been lucky.

He was the first German I'd spoken personally to all the war. Scruffy, wearing a genuine scuttle helmet under which was a chubby unfazed face, he didn't actually remark: "For us the war is finished" or the German equivalent, but everything about him expressed that happy thought. It was a pity he didn't have a general with him, we'd have got Brownie points for that — anyway, we searched him, took his pistol and gave him a smoke. He must have been about my Father's age, a bit on the stout side and smelling about as ripe as we did; but for me the thing was: here's an actual man, not just a target to be shot at — a man! It was the first time I'd thought of those guys in their field grey uniforms in that way — you're neither trained nor encouraged to feel like that. The thought hit me — not in a flash of epiphany exactly, but strongly enough to lodge as a notion I've never forgotten. Another crack in the carapace perhaps.

So it seemed the war had suddenly become even more personal. We smoked and talked — a bit of both languages — he dragging at the cigarette we'd given him as if he was trying to get smoke down to his boots: I wonder he didn't fall flat on his back, but evidently his lungs were still in good order — no mean achievement after the dreadful stuff the Germans smoked. His car was out of fuel, which was a pity as I fancied having a drive in an enemy staff car, so we walked amicably back to our positions and gave him over to the infantry for transporting to a POW cage. Before he went, I slipped him a handful of cigarettes. I thought he was going to cry. "*Danke, danke*" he gulped, and that was the last we saw of him. Maybe we all learned something that afternoon.

The only other thing that livened things up before operations came to an end was when we hit a mine on a track going from somewhere to nowhere — as far as we were concerned. Actually, I think we hit a large pile of mines, probably our friend Fritz's — because they removed most of our suspension on one side, and it was plain our tank wasn't going anywhere except on the back of a recovery vehicle. We hadn't formally christened the old girl, she was usually referred to as "s**t or bust" — so it was sad that in the end she bust. We made a fire and had a brew since all was quiet, and waited for somebody to pick us up. After a while a group of sappers pottered along, sweeping for mines (things often happened in that order): they joined us in a leisurely mug of tea, then swept around us — and found mines a couple of feet from our fire. It was that sort of day. Come to think about it — it was that sort of a war.

CHAPTER
TWENTY-SIX

Strange Summer

At 5a.m. on 5 May 1945, we received a memorable morning call from brigade:

> *No advance beyond present positions. No tactical moves unless ordered. B.B.C Newsflash confirmed The German Army on 21 A. G. front surrenders w.e.f 0800 hours 5 May.*

What music to the ear on a gorgeous spring morning, what a change from the pent moments of Orders Groups when a day's activities were designated. And that for us was that. We had a three-day start before the official surrender of the German armies at Luneburg Heath on 8 May, and for a blissful week or so we idled, drank too much and slept. In due course we put the tanks on transporters and travelled south to the Magdeburg area in Saxony, to hold a salient that stuck inconveniently into Russian-won territory; we were to occupy this area until such time as it was to be handed over to them. Politicians would probably have called it a Political Anomaly — for us it was to be mostly a pain.

However, there was just one more thing waiting for us. On the way south somewhere between the towns of Soltau and Celle, we passed close to the concentration camp at Bergen Belsen. We picked up the scent of the place before we got there as a pervasive taint on the wind; the camp had to some extent been cleaned up, but what we saw so briefly from a distance was disturbing, even though we had no knowledge of the sheer extent and implications of what had happened there and in similar camps. At the time it struck me as being unpleasant and unusual, but without particular significance; reaction was retrospective when later we heard what actually had happened there — and it took a long while to comprehend something of such enormity. It seemed perhaps, to be the war's last warning comment to us who so easily had passed it by — a demonstration of the deeper depths that humanity is capable of — suggesting that man needs to do a lot better than that if in the end, he deserves to survive.

Our salient was just a river's width from a fidgety Russian Army — an area of fearful civilians aware that before long we would leave — and the dreaded Russians would move in, a likely sentence of rape and violence, and probably worse. The tension wasn't eased much by the weather, hot and mosquito-laden, brooding over a countryside dotted with deserted half-destroyed factories and near-empty villages.

Every day we ran a patrol of tanks along our side of the Elbe, uncomfortably aware that Russian binoculars were tracking every yard of our progress. It was tinder dry, just needing a spark to get things going. Despite that, time dragged — there's a limit to the amount of maintenance one can do on a tank; there was little to do, and all day to do it in; we couldn't even swim as the river was polluted with things beyond imagination, together with the too frequent passage of bodies bobbing and twirling in its currents — one passing with a supplicating arm sticking out of the water — definitely drowning, not waving. We sat around and sweated bad temperedly in what shade we could find; with little to occupy us, reaction was beginning to set in.

For something to do I began cross-country running again. A few friends and I went out in the evenings when it was cooler, following remote tracks that seemed to dawdle for ever through land scarred and rough as the pelt of some exhausted creature asleep in the not quite stillness. Woodlands aren't a big feature in that part of Saxony, so we weren't unduly cautious about where we went, usually taking a route of five miles or so round our village. But we were mindful of the times and I never ran without my Smith & Wesson strapped alongside, a perpetual nuisance slap-slapping against my thigh — but a necessary friend.

As the time for our withdrawal and the arrival of Russian units came closer, there was a panic clearout of documents from a small factory close by, a clearout in which we participated: "sensitive documents" we were told — and for days the place was thick with smoke and agitated Germans, an agitation which increased as time grew shorter. Plainly the locals were increasingly terrified at the prospect of Russian occupation, such was the reputation gained during their long advance westwards. The locals were desperate to be allowed to leave with us — but orders were clear: all civilians were to stay put — and on a specified date we were to move out and head for Hanover, our next posting. I think we all felt bad about abandoning the place, such were the attitudes towards everything Russian at the time — a view that had taken hold with astonishing speed even at our level, and it's not surprising that Churchill's Iron Curtain dropped so quickly to divide Europe for the next forty something years.

Eventually the day came; we got on the waiting transporters and headed north. Nobody had much to say as we perched on our tanks and enjoyed the breeze; there was even less to say when we spotted the dust of the approaching Russian units — two worlds — already at odds. Our meeting seemed like a film in slow motion: two victorious armies that had fought as allies over pretty much the whole of Europe, briefly en passant — but without greeting, change of pace or expression on the bearded faces of the soldiers crammed into their beat-up trucks. They were led by a staff car, followed by the muscle of a T34 tank with its sloping sides and supple suspension — first glimpse for us of a tank famous for the part it played in battles such as Kursk and elsewhere. The encounter took less than five minutes and left nothing in its wake except the settling dust and a sense of foreboding. I didn't think of it at the time, but it was an ironic situation — beat one enemy, get another free. What a bargain.

CHAPTER
TWENTY-SEVEN

Dives

So summer gave us Hanover — and Hanover looked as if the horsemen of the Apocalypse had arrived, done the business and moved on. The sheer enormity of what total war involves was everywhere brutally apparent on a grand scale — and from what I saw there and elsewhere, the sharpest edge of war had been borne, as usual, by civilians. A battle is a battle — usually a relatively limited convulsion — on the other hand, a thousand bombers attacking a city is a massacre, no less — the infamous destruction of Dresden in April 1945 being a prime example. In those early days little had been done to start the clearing-up, a task that was later effected with Teutonic efficiency in all the shattered towns and cities. Large areas of Hanover were still rubble, burial piles remaining as the bombs had left them, stinking in the sun: here were skeletal arches, walls and pillars at astonishing angles as if petrified by heat; what had become almost a cliché picture of a flight of stairs still with banisters clinging to a gaily papered wall — and seemingly everywhere were rathole alleyways leading into partially excavated limbo where people were living. And over everything hung the dry kiss of dust.

What struck me as being particularly incongruous was the fact that some streets had been partly cleared, with electricity restored and a few trams running again, bucking and grinding on still damaged tracks. Where they came from or went, I never discovered, and those not reserved for occupation forces were as amazingly overcrowded as trams anywhere else in Europe. What seemed particularly surreal was that it came across as a weird play being acted out — with Hanover as its stage. For years that street was the stuff of dreams for me: a theatre contrived from chaos, its players acting out the queue waiting to go shopping where there were no shops, no money and nothing to buy.

That was daytime, but the nights stirred something different. Human endeavour, spirit, or whatever you want to call it, doesn't lie dormant for long — and somehow the city was creaking still further into action again. The entrepreneur sees an opening: you're stuck with occupying troops who need entertaining, what entertains best? Drink, women and music, of course. Somehow nightclubs (perhaps an euphemism) began to grow like mushrooms in extraordinary places; partly wrecked buildings were somehow shored-up, cellars that had withstood the weight of a wrecked building were miraculously equipped — often very imaginatively. You might find yourself sitting on an ammunition box at a sawn off barrel that was serving as a table garnished with a weepy candle in a tin, and drink your beer from a milk bottle — one place used green frosted ones. It was best to stick to beer, though you could risk schnapps of a sort and other drinks — but there was a lot of wood spirit around, and who knew where it finished up — though a lot of people found out the hard way, the luckier ones winding-up in the notorious 29th British General Hospital elsewhere in Hanover.

One place of note had a piano nearly in tune and a leggy troupe of girls — well, not quite girls any more — decked out in a sort of can-can gear with feathers, who put on their smiles and miraculously got through their dance routines without actually falling off the end of a miniscule stage. They were there to dance and anything else required of them, with a tariff for pretty well everything — and they certainly would have had to pay the jovial proprietor his cut for the privilege.

The dive, and you more or less had to do that to get in, was hot, smoke-laden and noisy — a study in blacks, scarlet and garish orange — as basic as you could get maybe, but still a focus of life in a world of so much death. In those days real money was the cigarette: twenty would buy a lot and with a couple of hundred you could pretty well retire. With a defunct Mark and a dodgy (to Germans) military currency, cigarettes must have been more than a little influential in restarting the country's economy. Strange days indeed, days of yet another phoenix slowly rising from its ashes — encouraging the hope that there's little that exists without the possibility of redemption.

At that time I had to visit Hamburg on some army business or other, and found that progress towards some sort of normality was happening there as well, as indeed it must have been going on everywhere else. Even the famed Reeperbahn appeared to be dusting itself off (perhaps an understatement), busily addressing the matter of re-establishing its international reputation. On the obverse of the coin were the waters of the outer and inner Alster lakes, stretches of incongruous tranquillity sporting an occasional flotilla of water birds, which evidently had the good sense to have wintered elsewhere, and noticeably keeping well away from the banks — evidently aware of a hungry population. It was an area that must have offered a bit of relief to Hamburg's inhabitants at the height of the bombing — at least you can't destroy lakes with explosive — much of which would have finished up in those placid sun-reflecting waters.

In contrast to that brittle world was the town of Einbeck, old and timbered, maybe fifty miles from Hanover and not far from the Hartz Mountains; it had lived dangerously, but by some quirk had survived untouched by bombing or armies. For a while we settled there after leaving Hanover, hooligans with tanks, first indulging in the must-have military parade that crunched the streets and did little for drains and old foundations. The population shorn of its young men, turned out to watch the pomp and ceremony; I recall them as we rumbled past, women holding their children — and beside them old men who had tasted it all before. Armies have the tact of bullocks, but at least we weren't Russians.

CHAPTER
TWENTY-EIGHT

Aftermath

One of the many problems of a country with its infrastructure destroyed and with only the Allied Control Commission, the CCG (irreverently known as Charlie Chaplin's Grenadiers) struggling to establish some sort of order, was the pressing matter of what to do with the thousands of displaced people, the DP's: these were the lost and desperate ones, uprooted by circumstance and invasion, forced into labour camps or prison, or just left stranded where they stood. Many of these DP's were Poles, both homeless and vengeful — and in that desperate summer many travelled in groups, surviving by violence, by rape and robbery, moving from village to village in the distant more vulnerable parts of a country that was the focus of their hate.

The Hartz Mountain region is more hilly than mountainous when compared with what lies in southern Germany, but it was still remote, heavily forested and perfect for those marauding groups, and not long after we had settled into our billets in Einbeck, we were landed with the task of providing a measure of protection for farms and villages in that area. And so on a hot summer's day, we found ourselves somewhat tentatively map reading our way off tarmac roads on to dusty tracks that climbed into dense country offering an occasional unlikely schloss perched on a spur protruding from the forest. The place was heavy with film images of vampire and werewolves, a niggling worry arising from lurid tales of ex-SS fanatics setting up resistance groups in unprotected areas to attack the occupying forces. Real or imagined, these groups — distinct from DP's — had been dubbed "werewolves", and had become an ongoing and much exaggerated bar topic among those who hadn't actually come across any — but knew someone who knew someone who had. Despite our reservations, I think we were just as edgy and alert as a crew, as we'd been in the fighting days.

Eventually we found our designated village — a few houses and farms hazy under a thin scarf of wood smoke, which were grouped as if for company on an island of open fields won from the forest. Our arrival, which set the dogs barking and the curtains twitching, was evidently a relief to the villagers who would have been uncomfortably aware of their vulnerability, and which probably accounted for the muted but relieved reception we received. We settled ourselves in an orchard that offered a strategic view over most of the dwellings, brewed up our compo tea and enjoyed the sun and the prospect of bit of peace and quiet.

We were there for a several weeks before we returned to Einbeck, and it was a pleasant interlude; food and mail arrived by truck a couple of times a week, and we were well away from Squadron HQ and its devoted purpose of finding everybody unnecessary jobs to do. It seemed like well-earned time out and we relished our own space, though we all did our turn at guard duty every night and carried our Sten guns and side arms at all times — with orders to use them if necessary. Night guard was as spooky as it had been in the fighting days when we were leaguered up somewhere and worrying about German patrols; as then, you did your time in the open turret chasing imaginary shadows you just knew hadn't been there before — and nerves couldn't be settled by a cigarette either, its glow can be spotted from a couple of hundred yards at least, and the smoke detected even further than that in still weather. From the start we did all the usual night-happy things with cocked weapons and finger on trigger, but were spared any real dramatics in the short dark summer hours.

Our village was a peasant community without its young men: those remaining were younger women and their children together with granny and grandpa — all living as they had always done, with the work around house or farm being everybody's work. If you were young you did the heavy jobs and grew something to eat; Grandpa sat under a tree smoking leaf and newspaper cigarettes and minded the precious flock of geese all the daylight hours (he took to our army Capstans with hardly a cough), while Grandma fussed over the children and made the soup. We weren't supposed to fraternise but we did, and got to know them and they us, almost with liking I think — particularly when they realised we really were there to protect them and weren't after the women — much as we would've liked to try our luck. That was a time when even the licentious soldiery was aware that these women had experienced more than enough hassle, and needed a bit of peace and quiet in a world where their only good luck was the fact of who we were.

We used our fractured German, swapped cigarettes and rations for eggs, while conversation flowered from small beginnings, and was often illuminating. For some, the war had cost them sons and husbands they still didn't know to be alive or dead and wouldn't know, maybe for years. Stalingrad, Kursk, Falaise, brought anguished responses and sometimes tears; these were people rooted in the earth and for them the war had robbed them of a future. I think they really had no idea about the camps of Auschwitz, Belsen or the others, insulated as they were by their terrain. War had skirted round them, sucked in their children and gone its blundering course — so they, the remaindered ones lived the way they'd lived for years: working, waiting, and minding their geese.

The forest was home to wild boar — fleet-footed swine with sharp tusks (as they were described to us); on more than one occasion they'd stood our hair on end during night guard with their grunting and snapping of twigs. One day some of us decided to have a boar shoot; leaving a few volunteers behind as guards, we set off early armed with an inappropriate selection of guns which included Stens and a couple of Schmeissers. The forest was a green stillness where no birds sang as we spread out along aisles of larch and pine, avoiding give-away twigs and mindful of DP's as well as resident boar. Despite our efforts, I think we

196

must have appeared as rank amateurs as far as the boar were concerned, since we didn't even hear a grunt all day — which was probably just as well if they were as fleet-footed and sharp as they had been described to us.

For me though, that day's hunting wasn't really the point of the exercise, I just enjoyed the sense of timelessness that had been so little disturbed by the extremes of violence in the world outside — a violence that had turned forest into a kind of sanctuary. Its scents were wonderful, an all-encompassing fragrance of resin and centuries of fallen pine needles; for once, being in the shadows of trees didn't constitute a threat, it seemed a release — and I even forgot the possibility of hostile DP's for a while.

After that summer I never heard of further attacks on villages, which was probably partly the result of action that had to be taken against the more aggressive of the wandering DP groups. On one occasion we were required to undertake a dismounted operation to flush out and hold a group known to be living in a disused factory not far from Einbeck. This was something completely new to us, an action that infantry wouldn't have thought twice about; it was a very early start and we were in position before first light with everybody nervously pussyfooting about and worrying. The situation seemed haunting and surreal; at a given signal we entered the dank building which must have been some sort of office block, and worked from room to room with our Stens cocked, rousing the sleeping occupants and giving them time enough only to collect such possessions as they could carry, before feeding them back to be escorted away. The action was remarkably slick, quiet and efficient. They had been sleeping rough on blankets and what looked like sacks — and from one tousled heap climbed two young men naked and shivering: some basics of the world evidently remained unchanged even in those crazy days.

That was an operation I hated to be part of, and I don't think anybody felt good about it; these people were the dispossessed with little more to lose, but I suppose it was a step in the direction of re-establishing some sort of order in a world temporarily without the controls of a normally policed society — it was a case of starting somewhere. This group was taken to a holding centre where they were to be sorted out — a near impossible task, I'd think. But in the end the job must somehow have been done — at least in practical terms, by way of repatriation or resettlement — although I'm sure the emotional side of their lives wouldn't have been repaired as easily as that. It was a brutal impersonal world — and I was grateful for being me

CHAPTER
TWENTY-NINE

Göttingen . . . and Lloyd George Knew My Father

Time spent in immediate post-war Germany was something of a limbo, a period of anti-climax regarded as an irritating obstacle to the business of getting on with your life — particularly by those who had been at it since 1939, and in that respect I counted myself lucky. The process of demobilisation was organised on a first in first out basis, fair — but taking many months to effect; it seemed to be a time of slack water and initially one of some uncertainty. For example, towards the end of 1945 the Sherwood Rangers, together with other redundant territorial units, was disbanded and its personnel distributed among regular regiments who were destined to have a much longer shelf life. Accordingly, some colleagues and I were posted for a few months to the 11th Hussars, an armoured car outfit which had been a part of the 7th Armoured Division in the days of strife. We weren't unduly impressed by the change, since we were tank men and

199

armoured cars were hardly a fitting substitute — but there was a major benefit. Being a regular cavalry regiment, in some miraculous way (one didn't ask how such things were managed in those days) they had assembled a very fine stabling of horses.

I had always enjoyed being on horseback, having ridden quite often from a stables on the Downs at home, and it wasn't long before I found myself being schooled in a very large covered arena by Walter, a former German Olympic competitor, who was a brilliant teacher with a particular weakness for schnapps; whoever fell off while we went round and round the ring, jumping with and without stirrups and other uncomfortable exercises, had to pay him a bottle of the stuff. I hate to think what it did to his liver, because I fell off at least a dozen times in various dramatic directions, as did everybody else. However, Walter — remarkably still on his feet — seemed fit enough, and by the time he'd finished with us we had become passable riders, which meant we were allowed to ride in the outside world. I remember wonderful canters in the snowy winter of 1946 when there were brass monkeys everywhere, and it was cold enough for there to be ice floes in the harbour at the Hook of Holland — a fact I noticed without enthusiasm when returning from UK leave.

At that time we were stationed near Helmstedt on the border of the Russian-occupied zone, and for a few weeks we officially "patrolled" a forested mile or two of the border itself on horseback — pure affectation of course, and I imagine the Russians on the other side of the border would have had a good laugh at such amateurs trying to do the Cossack thing in snowy wastes that, by their standards, must have been thought quite spring-like. At any rate, it was different and since nobody was shooting at us, it was fun — and after a couple of hours of exercise in the stinging cold, breakfast in the mess was a ravenous affair.

To be fair, occupation duties in post war Germany did have their good points and time could be whittled away until your number (literally) came up; another great asset was the fact that short leaves could be taken quite frequently in between the six-monthly UK privilege leaves (note the adjective — the army didn't want us to think we had any right to leave). These short breaks from routine seemed to be regarded as the "perks" of being stuck in a foreign country for years, and offered visits to leave centres in many places: Amsterdam, Paris, Copenhagen and Ihrwald in Austria were just some of the options. With the help of a friend who worked in squadron office and dealt with such vital commodities as leave passes and travel warrants, many opportunities presented themselves — a tacit arrangement of low profile and timing. So that period when most of the army seemed to be going home — except you, did have its moments. Having never been abroad before the war, this was new territory needing to be explored.

Travel was by train and I found trains exciting; you climbed up into them, they were dirty and smutty, but many still showed evidence of grander days — brass fitments, mahogany facings to doors and windows, and bell pushes that once had summoned your attendant from the dining car. These long exotic trains went to exotic places too; in the early days after the war the Nord Express, for a time, started from Calais and took you all the way, somewhat circuitously, to Copenhagen. It was pure pleasure to be travelling so easily and comfortably across territory that had taken so long to cover before. Much of it was as the war had left it; I remember seeing the fuselage of a Lancaster bomber nose down and somehow still held in place by supporting trees — miraculously it appeared not to have burned, and from a distance still looked undamaged — though surreal without its wings.

I was restless and up for anything and everything; I saw the most beautiful woman I've ever come across on the Nord Express to Copenhagen. She stopped my heart. At another time, another place, beauty was waiting on a platform deep in the Paris Metro — I took the next train back hoping to track her down — but unsurprisingly was too late (how mad can you get?). While skiing at the leave centre in Austria, I spent most of the time on my back in the snow with my skis crossed overhead, but the mountains with their peaks deep into a near-violet sky were totally beautiful; Berlin and Amsterdam were entertaining contrasts in what was becoming a habit-forming tour. Tempting educational courses were available too, so at last, sated with exotica and interesting contacts, and with my demob number coming ever closer, I put in for a teacher-training course being held in Göttingen. I had no intention of teaching then — that took years to come about — but the prospect of something different in a historic place appealed, and got me off the squadron hook for several weeks.

Göttingen had survived the war pretty well; I believe there had been a tacit understanding with the Germans, they didn't bomb Oxford or Cambridge and we didn't bother with Heidelberg or Göttingen — and the agreement must have held. As an old university town it was very much alive, with plenty of activities going on to lighten my ignorance of pretty well everything except war. I saw my first opera there — *Die Fledermaus*, a strange ad hoc affair with unstable scenery, dubious singers and a contralto of Wagnerian voice power and bosom. The evening was further enhanced by the sudden appearance of a stuffed, somewhat moth-eaten fledermaus, which was dropped heavily from the gods at exactly the wrong moment: everybody loved it.

In time off from our studies, which in the end taught me little about teaching, I went to concerts, tentatively visited libraries and began to look at the city's wealth of architecture with a new and appreciative eye. I don't know what I expected to find in Göttingen, which represented a world I hadn't really been aware of before. My twenty or so years had treated mainly with the physical and modern, even Lancing with its trappings could boast less than a century of existence, though I had explored the rounds of some of English antiquity with my parents. What I was seeing and wandering through struck me as different — or more likely perhaps, my sensibilities were operating differently. The city seemed small, secret and — Other . . . that quality used by D.H Lawrence (as I later learned), to illuminate the abstract qualities of his world.

Cleansed to twentieth-century standards, no ordure issued from upper windows, no red kites (did old Germany have red kites?) picked at the unspeakable on the streets: yet imbued with that haunting otherness, Göttingen suggested all that had ceased but a few moments ago, that the last plague cart had only just disappeared round the corner, and at any minute a pompous procession of academe in full regalia would solemnly appear. Needing no nosegay, the place seemed to have taken centuries and wars in its stride — and looking back, I think the short period I spent there was the catalyst, albeit premature, suggesting that one day I would be ready for something new. It had struck me so strongly as being an island that had risen above the taint of the Nazi years. I was drawn by what it seemed to offer, its apparent quietude of thought, making it a place of the metaphysical as well as the physical — though that was certainly a concept I couldn't have expressed in such terms at the time.

As a final bonus — and one pretty much out of context with everything else I'd been soaking up during my stay, I happened on the film of *Henry V* in an out-of-place army cinema, to be carried away by Henry's (played by Laurence Olivier) reception of the Dauphin's gift of tennis balls, later to applaud the intensity and volume of the English archers' flighted barrage into the armour of advancing French knights at

Agincourt — noting that the fundamentals of battle don't change much. It was light years removed from those hours of classroom Shakespeare at school; not quite sated by all I'd been soaking up during my stay — I wanted more.

Göttingen was, in a sense, the end of a journey of many facets — one that came up in the end with an illuminating insight to another way of thinking that was to become an important part of my life; ironically this small renaissance emanated from what not long before had been deep in the heartland of an enemy we'd been fighting for nearly six years. It's a funny old world.

Eventually, late in 1947 my demob group came up, and by way of the Hook of Holland and Harwich, I arrived in York to be documented and kitted out as a civilian again. Duly processed like something dropped off a conveyor belt, I emerged with my precious discharge documents and a cardboard suitcase of new clothes, plus an unwanted trilby hat which I donated off the head, so to speak, to a surprised porter on the platform at York station. Even more eventually, I caught a crowded night train to London with a lot of other bemused neo-civilians.

I arrived at Victoria Station very early and had to wait for a milk train back to Eastbourne, spending the time in a stuffy euphemistically entitled refreshment room furnished with yellow oilcloth on the tables and three pickled eggs huddled under a glass cover on the counter. I shared a table with an obvious demob survivor who evidently had been refreshing himself for some considerable time; by the look of his ribbons he'd

205

done Africa and Italy as well as my little bit, so I felt he was entitled to such small indulgences. Precariously tilting his chair, he remarked with alcoholic solemnity — "Lloyd George knew my Father", and burped.

"Father knew Lloyd George" I replied, remembering the church parade where I'd first heard that interesting but somewhat repetitive variation on a familiar hymn. We grinned at each other and relaxed. We'd never met before, would most likely never meet again, but we had one important thing in common — we'd made it home.

CHAPTER
THIRTY

Banks and New Beginnings

Coming back from abroad to be a civilian wasn't easy, despite all the years dreaming about it. From the interesting times that had gone before, I had learned several affecting things — probably the most striking of which was the growing realisation that, along with everybody else, I had been merely an expendable item — a notion that had been staring me in the face since school, but one I hadn't fully registered until relatively recently; in fact, it must have been sparked by the conversation I described earlier with Brigadier Horrocks. Now distanced and in different circumstances, it was an illumination to play with — allowing imagination full rein: people as animated ordnance, for instance. *Monty Python* might have done something with that.

With hindsight and a modicum of thought, it became apparent that reaction to the calculated business of using lives to achieve, or not achieve, desired national ends, was a path well trodden by many before me, with Wilfred Owen putting final touches to the sense of outrage shared by many:

207

My friend, you would not tell with such high zest
To children ardent for some desperate glory,
The old lie: *dulce et decorum est*
Pro patria mori.

Which of course was the same high zest we'd been
nurtured on, and there we were as ardent as anything
— small wonder we all dropped off the end of the
conveyor belt singing. So there it was — if you were
lucky as I was, you came home and got on with your
life — if you weren't, your home became a box of bones
lined-up in some immaculate military cemetery,
elsewhere to be recorded by yet another place on the
Roll Of Honour Board your school is so proud of. I
resolved then that no children of mine were going to be
wasted like that, if I had anything to do with it.

It occurred to me during that unsettled leave time,
that I might have a shot at writing something about the
previous four years that had changed me pretty rapidly
from a boy to something else. I liked the idea, made
some false starts — but the necessary skills of
expression and assimilation I realised just weren't there,
and more practically — though it's a feeble excuse —
there was little private space to work in at home and the
cavernous town library was full of old men coughing
and rustling newspapers. So the idea withered and went
into what was to be a very long hibernation, leaving me
with the more immediate — and rather exciting —
prospect of getting some sort of future together —
perhaps even earning a living.

So Göttingen, touchstone to things that were going to be important to me later on, and seeming to be another world a very long way from home, went under mental wraps for a while. The prospect of ninety days' leave calculated on time spent abroad, together with plenty of petrol coupons, became absorbing diversions. We unearthed our hibernating car, which had languished under covers in the garage since 1939, and my parents got behind the wheel again after years of abstinence, while I concentrated on keeping to the left side of the road — something I wasn't at all used to. Money and mobility made me a popular item, and I enjoyed the resurrected hotels and nightspots that were slowly giving Eastbourne new life. There was plenty of company and many like me, not long back and clueless about what to do next; we drank too much and tried our luck with English girls — an absorbing occupation for us all.

Without doubt, resurrection was the word. Eastbourne had picked itself up to become a very different proposition from the sad down-at-heel place full of *angst* and air raid sirens I'd left to join the army early in 1944; much had been achieved in a couple of years since the war ended, and not just a lick of paint either. Bourne Street where we'd played our Sunday Home Guard games, had been cleared and rebuilding was in progress — and Terminus Road was pretty well as I remembered it from before 1939; many of the old shops had reappeared as if by magic, and there were new ones to add a bit more gloss — remember the *John Collier, John Collier — the window to watch* advertisement? It was a trendy men's outfitter that was to take my money for years. Then there was my Father's bombed bank at 115 Terminus Road, grandly restored to space and dignity — but without its bomb-receptive dome.

Of course, one can't forget the cinemas, still in pole position before television arrived — refurbished and busy showing in glorious Technicolor just how Douglas Fairbanks and Errol Flynn had won the war practically single-handed, while David Niven fresh from Pinewood Studios, still with his fine-line moustache, battled bravely on in crippled bombers. You could still get a game of tennis at the Devonshire Park grass courts, which host the pre-Wimbledon big names today; then there was dancing to a swinging live orchestra in the Winter Garden ballroom at teatime, with another session later — and if you had any energy left in the evening, you could take in a Will Hay drama in the theatre.

Despite the fact that nationally it was a tighten your belt time of "export or die", there were a few new cars beginning to be seen around the streets and preening on the promenade — just a few examples like the sexy little Sunbeam Talbot that made our old hearse of a Morris look like, well — an old hearse. And there were a few enterprising restaurants putting up stripy awnings and tempting menus too — and I'd guess they did well, because food was still big in our lives, anywhere you could get a steak (I still think of those early post war steaks in reverential terms), was a Mecca to me.

Yes, slowly but surely things were looking up — and in those irresponsible days before reality kicked in, Eastbourne was a good place to be — especially if you were lucky enough to have both opportunity and time on your hands. It's beautiful too; climb the twisty road from Holywell at the end of the promenade, and you'll come eventually to a secluded area overlooking the golf course, it's known as Paradise — a place of opportunity most appropriately named, I always thought. Or you could drive on up to Beachy Head itself and park near the deserted coastguard cottages; at night you have a wonderful vista of the coast all the way round to Hastings twinkling with lights — so romantic.

I remember one evening while a companion and I were busily admiring the view, a police car stopped nearby and a constable came over to enquire — having first flashed his torch searchingly into our car — whether we'd seen a fire engine pass recently. A fire engine? As well expect a hearse or milk float to be out on a deserted Beachy Head at 1a.m. Do you think he might have had misgivings about us?

London had its attractions too. For 17s 6d you could buy a return ticket from Eastbourne to Victoria and the delights beyond; the journey took an hour and twenty minutes each way — probably quicker than today — so an evening's jaunt was easily possible. Like Eastbourne, the place was putting itself back together again — although there were still many partly cleared bomb-damaged areas, some with a welcome splash of bright ragged robin flowers and buddleia bushes, both

211

of which seemed especially to relish those wrecked sites as rock gardens, and did a lot to brighten them up.

London as always, was swinging; a favourite expedition for me was a visit to Lei On's — a brilliant Chinese restaurant not far from Victoria; Chinese food was still a bit of a novelty then, and it was a popular place. Theatres were going strong too — with *Oklahoma* a top billing, or for something less robust there was always an offering from Ivor Novello to tempt — and of course there were the pubs, and even more Hollywood war films to tell it like it was. Those early days after demob were fabulous days for me, with time and space and a bit of money to splash. Yes, for a while tomorrow could look after itself. And I let it.

Eventually of course, reality prevailed — well it had to sooner or later. Living with my parents had proved not to be a good idea, too much a collision of worlds I suppose — but also at that time they were having relationship problems and I got in the way — particularly as I was a very different person from the one who took off for Glasgow years before, and probably seemed more of a stranger than a son — just one more thing for them to cope with. After six years of war everybody had to adjust, the dynamics of pretty well everything being different — and families weren't exempt. Father, probably in desperation, suggested I give banking a try — so with no better ideas and with leave money beginning to run short, I agreed. With his influence getting a job wasn't a problem, and before long I found myself working as a junior clerk at a branch of Barclays Bank in Eastbourne.

It wasn't my bag. To me the whole routine of shuffling cheques and chasing elusive figures to make columns balance was frustrating and tedious. Father had become manager at another Eastbourne branch by then, and one or two of the senior staff where I was working, weren't above having the odd jibe at what they called my privileged position. One particular character fingered the cloth of my sports jacket (we were allowed casual dress on Saturday mornings) and speculated aloud how pleasant it must be to be well connected and able to afford such quality. He never knew how close he'd been to concussion and a handful of broken fingers — fortunately my fuse though short, wasn't that short, and anyway there was Father to consider. But it was close.

I did a few months of that, bought a motorbike — a shiny silver and black machine that was positively slow by today's standards — and burned up the still nearly empty roads over the Downs and sometimes far away; but I missed the brute bulk and complexities of Shermans and tried to compensate by taking the bike to bits at weekends. In the meantime I started to go out with Mary whose home was close to mine, but who was nursing at St Thomas's Hospital in London at the time, so initially our relationship was spasmodic, being limited to occasional weekends. But even in the early days she made a difference, and I slowly cooled down and became less self-focused — not before time, I think.

Mary was to be a turning point in my life. When I first saw her it had been one of those rare moments of illumination — that shooting star feeling — when something inside you says, "You're the one!" and after that nothing is quite the same; I was to do that just one more occasion many years later. She had been away in London most of the time, and on that first meeting had come home with a boy friend to join her sister and me for a dinner dance. I don't think it was one of those eye-to-eye meetings that explode across the proverbial crowded room, but something had sparked between us — and we danced together more than we should have done that evening.

CHAPTER
THIRTY-ONE

A Farming Year

One way and another it was watershed time. I left the bank and started work as a dogsbody on a small dairy farm; Father had a hand in that too, as the owner of the farm was a customer of his, and in those days customers were happy to oblige their bank managers on a quid pro quo basis. The farm was not far from the village of Hooe, which once dipped its feet in the sea — and had been the haunt of smugglers; now it sits back on higher ground a couple of miles inland, looking over the Pevensey Marshes — and its pub the Red Lion proved to be a much used watering hole for us on hot working days.

This time the enterprise worked out for me, largely because it was my first taste of real country, and I was turned on by the marshes and the rising landscape of the Sussex Weald as it stretched away northwards, wooded and interspersed with corn fields — one of which I remember wore a bright slash of poppies like a wound. In my Bexhill days, we had lived out of town — but it wasn't the same, being close to the coast with acres of scrubby ground that one day was to be built on, and was far removed from well-ordered fields carrying their crops and livestock. Cattle were something I had seen from time to time, often dead, but this was hands-on contact with a new world, and I found it good. For a start I lived at home and motorbiked every day over the marshes from Eastbourne — a pleasure in itself on an early morning with cattle floating like ghosts in mist rising from the dykes: it was great wind-in-the-face stuff — I could have been Biggles with my flying helmet and goggles!

With Archie, Bernard and Harry, the regular farm workers, I put the hours in and learned a lot of new things — sometimes with time enough to lark about with Ellen, a former land girl given to tight sweaters and jodhpurs, who when she wasn't larking about, was in charge of the Jersey herd with their pretty dished faces and sexy eyes; she sang to them sometimes and they milked like anything. It was a very feminine part of the farm activities. Archie had done the infantry thing in Normandy and points further on, and sometimes of an evening we would sit in the public bar of the Red Lion and get argumentative over our pints — playing the game of bickering about the uselessness of tanks/infantry when it came to the crunch: but we both knew the answers to all that and got on well. Afterwards I'd run him home on the pillion of my motorbike — and if his face was really, really, white when he fell off outside his house, I knew the evening had been up to scratch.

Old (he probably wasn't, but looked the part) Harry was the farm carter who fussed over Flossie, a beautiful Shire horse with a very sweet tooth, that pulled anything not allocated to the little grey Ferguson tractor, which was the latest thing in those days — and very much the province of Bernard who didn't encourage outsiders like Archie and me to use it. Harry always smoked an antique pipe, a permanent facial feature except for daily excavation and decoking sessions. I got to know both Harry and Flossie well while we were weeding between the rows of mangolds with the horse shim — I led Flossie while Harry steered the shim with his pipe upside down and a drip on the end of his nose.

Harry was a character representing the end of an era. However hot the weather, he always wore his standard rig: woollen vest, flannel shirt, waistcoat, a tweed jacket and thick trousers tied as often as not at the knees with binder twine. He had endless stories, mostly apocryphal I think, and there weren't many farming skills he'd missed out on. At threshing time he was at his best, Flossie had a day off and Harry would do the rick building — it was loose straw in those days and slippery after threshing, but he paraded like an admiral on his poop deck, pitch-forking away and telling everybody what to do.

Those long threshing days were hard sweaty work focused entirely on the vast and roaring threshing machine in its strange livery of farm pink, the long belt flexing and slapping at the pulleys, the driving tractor bouncing on huge tyres and stinking of paraffin. You weren't reckoned to have done any farming at all until you'd threshed out a dozen stacks — flat-out days that had you knackered, half-deafened and coated with dust

217

by the time the last sheaves had gone through. Great times though, offering the excitement of getting to the bottom of a stack with the terriers all tensed-up and quivering, waiting for the rats to come out.

One evening at about sunset, the rats came out in a sudden concerted rush — and the terriers moved in on them in yapping delight; in the ensuing mayhem one of the smaller rats, desperate for cover, ran right up Bernard's trouser leg. To the best of my knowledge, vertical take-off was invented there and then by Bernard, who ascended at least 10ft yelling and clutching at his vital parts. It made our day — if not Bernard's — and proved Harry's point about tying binder twine round your trouser legs below the knees: I saw it as offering sensible damage limitation at least, and never threshed again without it. Neither did Bernard.

There was the same excitement when we were harvesting the oats and barley: with Flossie doing the work and lathered with sweat, Harry was charioteer on the binder (those were pre-combine days) with its sails revolving and the sheaves spilling out as it roared and clattered round and round the field in shimmering heat, the air thick as pollen and windless. But heavens, the thistles in those sheaves! They were an ever-present torture as we stood them up into the stooks that had to stay out in the field to hear the church bells of three Sundays before being carted in for stacking.

By evening there would be a small area left uncut, a miniature of the field's shape, and the last of the standing corn would be jumping and swaying as the trapped rabbits and hares ran this way and that vainly trying to find a safe way out. Then everybody would take up strategic positions with a gun, with Harry yelling "You'm be bloody careful with them guns — you hear me!" — for him this was something of a ritual as there was nobody around he didn't trust, though the first time I was there he did keep a weather eye on me. Like a stage set for drama, this scene was something rooted in history from those days when the prospect of an addition to the pot came seldom, and was a more than welcome prospect for a family.

By that time I had found lodgings in the village with Walter, a market gardener and his wife and young son: they were great people; hospitable and kind, fundamental to the village where Walter had lived since he was a boy. The other plus was that they lived conveniently close to the pub. Sometimes after work I'd give him a hand with picking-out young plants in his greenhouses, and he'd talk about how it had been in that part of Sussex in wartime, about Home-Guarding and keeping an eye on the great ghostly spaces of marshland at night — where once the Normans had slipped in with the tide on their way to Hastings. They still came in at particular times, Walter told me with certainty, you hear them beaching on the shingle, you hear the horses — and I believe him, remembering the resonance of my long-struck bell.

The year I moved into the world of agriculture was one of the best I've lived. We worked long hours for not much money in all weathers, at times when Sussex was at its beautiful best, and through taxing days when sea, marsh and sky blended to become a lowering pall, with the rain falling vertically. Those were days when Britain badly needed homegrown food to help the balance of payments problems still existing after the war. And farming then was labour intensive — unlike today; our hundred or so acres fully occupied four workers as well as Reginald, the owner — and still found room for me; everybody was an expert (I don't include myself!), and the farm demonstrated that fact. A ploughed field after Harry and Flossie had finished with it, looked immaculate; an Archie layered hedge was, well — beautiful. Bernard did his tractoring, which was skilled and various — and as I've said, Ellen made the Jerseys milk like anything. And they all passed something on to me, so that even I — as someone remarked when I left to go to college — had just about become a mite useful.

Meanwhile, Mary and I were getting to know each other; our relationship was developing and we met some weekends, maybe to eat out and dance — something you did in those days, especially dance. For 7s 6d you could have a four-course dinner and dance to Harry Loveday's live music at Eastbourne's Grand Hotel — and grand it was, complete with aspidistras and bejewelled old ladies with blue hair occupying the Palm Court and looking at you disapprovingly. They were monkey-suit events with the girls in long dresses, and the plushy sophistication of those Saturday evenings seemed an enormous jump from mangold bashing with Harry on a frosty morning when my fingers resembled swollen sausages about ready to drop off with the cold: I was living in two worlds, but the contrast suited me fine — and anyway I was seriously in love by then.

At home things had evolved as they often do, and a stay over Saturday night proved to be about right for my parents as well as me: in small doses they loved me and I them. It must have been a hard time for them both — for Mother in particular: she was I think, feeling insecure and was not enthusiastic about the physical side of marriage. Father needed what was not provided and had an eye for women anyway — in that field he had few problems. He was good-looking, well mannered, and in his quiet way really did love women in the widest sense. He also occupied an enviable position in the town at a time when a bank manager even of a small branch, had both clout and a certain charisma. So the problems were real — especially for Mother, who was not able to react in kind, or didn't want to. In the 1940s and 50s, days before equality of the sexes became notionally the norm, divorce was social death for a woman — with separation almost as dire. It was a man's world still.

In the end, my parents worked things out and settled into a relationship which lasted over sixty years: they needed breathing space and made good use of it in facing up to the realities of settling back to the everyday after six years of ongoing disruption. Nowadays their difficulties would probably have been attributed to post war stress — with offers of counselling maybe. Post-traumatic stress hadn't been invented then for the services, let alone anybody else: if you were damaged and stressed-out as millions were, you got on with it as

221

best you could. In those days war was a very different beast from what it is today, and stress arising from it often took years to sort out.

CHAPTER
THIRTY-TWO

Back to School

In 1949 with millions recently demobilised, there were few places at university or college not already taken up — but in any case I was then light years away from being academically up to a university education. I had to grow into that much later on; so rather tentatively, I applied for a place at Plumpton Farm Institute near Lewes in Sussex for a one-year general agricultural course — and amazingly was accepted. To obtain a place you had to have worked for a year on a farm to gain some practical experience, and by the summer I had completed this requirement.

So September 1949 saw me happily installed at the Half Moon pub in Plumpton village, complete with motorbike and good intentions to become an earnest hard-working student. College policy was to accommodate only younger students on campus, old sweats like me had to find alternative slots — and Plumpton's delightful and accommodating pub was an opportunity waiting to happen. Much was I envied! Les Downey the landlord and his wife were delighted, if a little bemused, by what had hit them — since at a stroke their pub became a meeting place for the detritus of several of the demobbed services, not only a focus of our activities, but a centre for much of the village — as well as casuals who came to view what, in effect, was an ongoing mess party doing its thing for the better part of a not very academic year. Everybody adapted very happily, and I don't suppose the pub's business had ever been so good.

Mrs Downey, who looked as if she was something that had dropped off the jolly bulk of her husband, very much enjoyed her "little nips", and most evenings around 9p.m., she'd be more than ready for bed. Leaving us all to it, she'd disappear from the scene — but before she did, she always prepared supper on a tray which she put in my room upstairs for safety. Next morning at breakfast (if I was up to breakfast) she would be absolutely normal, fussing about and asking if the party had gone well and would I like more tea? I think I must have stirred the maternal in her, because I deserved none of her kindnesses and generosity.

By that time though, relations had cooled off between Mary and me: it was nothing dramatic but we both felt we needed a bit of space. Mary went off to Brighton to start her midwifery training, and I devoted myself to the rigours of life at agricultural college. From both our points of view that separation seemed a sensible thing, and we were both pretty sanguine about it. I don't remember how Mary felt about our relationship at the time, but it never occurred to me that such separation was going to be permanent: as I saw it, matters were merely in abeyance while we got ourselves together.

On a general agricultural course you did a mix of classroom and practical work on the very extensive farm run by the college, while weekends were largely devoted to sport and serious bar work. The academic staff were apparently put out by what they saw as the unfortunate mix of students who sat at their feet — the ex-service element being felt to be a disruptive influence on the impressionable younger ones. Probably they were justified, since we were inclined to quibble and argue and didn't conform to traditional attitudes of respect; fundamentally I think the problem was that we had changed and they hadn't — and nobody gave much ground.

There was a particular lecturer known as Kipperfeet who irritated us as much as we irritated him; one evening matters came to a head when his car, a little Morris Minor, was lifted bodily by willing hands to be placed with precision between two trees that offered space only a foot or so longer than the car itself: it was a silent, careful job and no damage was done to car or trees. Much fury ensued, alarms and excursions exploded like fireworks, while the younger students watched happily amazed: such a thing, worse even than the traditional knickers on the flagpole! And who might have done it? The beastly old sweats must surely have been in the pub where they usually were — even the staff half-believed that, since it was an ongoing bone of contention.

Ultimatums were issued and ignored, suspicion prevailed and the situation bubbled and simmered like a kettle on its hob — and in the meanwhile poor

Kipperfeet had to walk. In the end the old sweats did the decent thing by volunteering to help out. It would take, as we pointed out, a dozen strong backs to sustain and extricate such a weight — but regardless of strain and the risk of injury, we would do it. And we did. Strangely — or maybe not so strangely, staff-student relations improved considerably after that unusual occurrence, perhaps a late recognition by everybody concerned, ourselves included, that it's not a good idea to push things too far.

The proximity of Brighton — "London by Sea" — with its theatres, shops, its two piers loaded with "What The Butler Saw", and heaven knows what other attractions, was more than a trifling temptation to us, and sometimes we cut practical work for a trip to that metropolis. The appeal of a morning's muck shovelling came as a poor second to the prospect of a stroll along the promenade to take in the health-enhancing benefits of sea air before, perhaps, a visit to the Old Ship Hotel for a noggin. Transport was assured — and with a friend on the pillion of my bike, I'm not very ashamed to admit that we indulged ourselves — salving our consciences by always being back in time for afternoon classes. It was hard for the farm manager to keep tabs on the practical work situation, there was a lot of farm and more students than he could have shaken several sticks at, so we were on to a pretty safe thing.

Actually we put in a lot of practical work on the farm, because even we realised that such hands-on experience was vital if we were going to make anything of our farming future; so on those lovely Sussex greensand acres, I came to grips with the basics of ploughing and the rare intricacies of layering a hedge. There were all the other matters you need to have a grasp of too: when is hay ready to cut? And cart? Is this ear of wheat ripe enough to harvest? You smell and feel, rub the ear between the palms of your hands, bite and test it under the eye of a man who's been doing it for decades. In those fascinating days I learned much of what I needed to provide myself with the necessary background — and it's lucky I did, since much of what I learned was crucial when later Mary and I were farming on our own account.

Most of us had played cricket at school so it wasn't hard to put together a competent side, which opened-up some interesting college fixtures. I recall a hot summer of matches on some lovely cricket grounds, Ditchling in Sussex among them. Our fortunes and fixtures were various: at Ditchling we played a combined Oxbridge touring side and beat them, on another occasion we played the local Plumpton team, and lost. I remember that game with affection — the pitch was diabolical and loaded with weeds that made the ball shoot unpredictably. Plumpton batted first and we got them out for something like seventeen runs; metaphorically rubbing our hands we batted and were dismissed for about twelve, it was that sort of game — and one that had to be continued in the Half Moon, together with most of the village.

My friends were all rugby players, and to be with them in the season I had to convert from the football I had played at Lancing. Fortunately, this turned out to be a relatively easy transition, allowing me to become a rugger-bugger and put on a scrumcap and get stuck into the scrum for Horsham that winter. Those were blissful days — we did our studies, worked as hard as necessary on the farm, drank far too much — and for once in my adult life, girls featured hardly at all. I think we were too old and unattractive for the female students, but in any case our energies were directed elsewhere. It was a time of catharsis, a time for doing the stupid mind-blowing wonderful things that young men do when they're back from the jungle.

Towards the end of the year, sometime in early summer I think, a letter from Mary arrived suggesting we might get together again. So we did — and picked-up our relationship as if there'd been no interruption. That period apart had worked its magic and for once in a way I had read a situation correctly. It was good timing too: Plumpton days were coming to an end with another phase waiting, and it was the same for Mary who had finished at Brighton and was due back in London. To add icing to the cake, I did well in college finals with a first class certificate and distinction in bookkeeping — much to my and everybody's surprise. Bookkeeping? Me? Must have been the beer.

CHAPTER
THIRTY-THREE

Is That a Proposal?

In the early days of our getting back together, Mary and I were still preoccupied with our work, but although she was back at St Thomas's in London, we did manage to see each other most weekends. She was busy getting used to ward routines again after a year or so doing the midwifery rounds in Brighton, and I was settling back into the so-called real world post-Plumpton era. As far as that real world was concerned, I was lucky to have had my place at the same farm held open for me, which meant I was spared the business of trying to find a job somewhere else — no easy task at that time. Anyway, it was really no hardship for me to slot in again with people I knew and liked, though I did get some stick from Archie and Bernard who enjoyed calling me "professor" and asking daft questions with very serious faces.

For a few months life went on as before — relaxed and pleasant, and I found rather to my surprise, that I had actually learned more than I had imagined from time spent on that large very well-run farm at Plumpton; another plus was the fact that Walter and his wife still had a spare room for me in the village. Not long after this, an opportunity to take on the management of a larger neighbouring farm came up. I applied for and was offered the post, which was one of responsibility as well as providing an improved salary of £6 a week — a joke by today's standards, but in 1950 it made the prospect of marrying viable.

It seemed a good time to get things going. Mary had been daft enough to accept my proposal of marriage, so the next step was to see what her Father thought about it — an obligatory move in those days, since you didn't just walk off with a daughter without permission. I imagine the occasion was set-piece stuff with everybody primed; one evening I was invited to their house, to be met by an anxious Mary, who with Mother and everybody else, promptly disappeared — leaving Father and I looking at each other. It was a set piece as I remarked, and one requiring a sports' jacket and tie, plus an extra shave as I had a heavy beard in those days — but it was a necessary performance that luckily ran its course without any of the problems a stage farce would require. I liked the Father in the plot and we had always had an easy relationship; he had done well in the First World War and had subsequently prospered in the fishing-tackle business, and evidently approved of me, though looking back I wonder why. So we played our parts until the lurking family eventually disengaged from the keyhole, and the job was done.

And in due course that is what we did. On 21 April 1951, on a bright and windy day, we married in St Mary's Church in Eastbourne's Old Town, later to have the reception at the Cavendish Hotel, all very smart and loaded with more of our parents' friends than ours. It was a lengthy and generous send-off, but we were relieved finally to climb into my little yellow MG that in the interests of marriage had supplanted my much-loved two wheels, pause to shake the confetti from practically everywhere, and get going to Folkestone and our first night — which in those days really was a first night. Not too early next morning, we took the boat to Calais and travelled by train to Lugano where we were due to spend the first week of our honeymoon.

Six years after the war continental train travel had gone up in the world, providing couchettes and a dining car, and everything was clean — more than a touch different from my earlier excursions. And all that with a wife! We dined that evening speeding across Europe watching a late sun work magic on straw stacks Monet might have painted in fields misty with distance, passed elegant lines of poplars admiring themselves in the looking glass of a lake, and watched a group of Frenchman leading their horses home from the fields — only Frenchmen wear berets like that.

I slept fitfully that night; once we stopped at some cavernous station, Strasbourg I think. I stuck my head out of the window into dank station air loud with clattering of trolley loads of milk churns: at 3a.m. mystery rules, where are those waiting figures going at such an hour? A porter with red piping round his cap studied me as he passed with a lantern in his hand, then our engine sighed and strained us slowly away. It was a world apart, one I had visited often enough on my travels as a soldier, but that early morning was

231

different. I had Mary, dead asleep under a scratchy blanket, and that changed everything. I slept until we reached Switzerland.

Honeymoons like holidays can be tricky: we had a stupid fight over some postcards, for a day or two it rained a lot — and once or twice we looked speculatively at each other with thoughts like — who is this person? What have I done? But we soon relaxed, the sun came out over the lake and things were right again. In that first week we were inveigled into taking a coach trip to Milan, the main attraction of which was its cathedral — of enormous Gothic stature, grey and gloomy — but humming with the crowds of local people who popped in, had a quick gossip, lit a candle or two before disappearing, something that appealed to us: a cathedral actually being used as part and parcel of everyday life.

We travelled to Interlaken in the Bernese Oberland for our second week and luckily the weather improved; we sailed on busy steamers criss-crossing Lake Thun under brooding mountains, watched of an evening men in *lederhosen* yodelling and blowing monstrous 10ft horns at us while we soaked up tiny glasses of cherry brandy. It was a boozy time we both needed and enjoyed. But what lay uncomfortably in the back of my mind was a niggling worm of worry about the Korean War which was still in full swing at the time. I was still an army reservist then — you were stuck with that as a matter of course for some considerable time after demobilisation, and I'd heard the military were thinking of calling-up reservists — avoidance of which

232

could mean all kinds of hassle for those who thought as I did.

It's funny how news you don't want to know about is always stuck under your nose, that time at breakfast for instance, by way of yesterday's *Daily Mail* with headlines an inch high, propped against the croissants on a table opposite — sufficient almost to put me off that luscious black cherry jam the Swiss do so well, along with their cuckoo clocks. "Don't gloom," instructed Mary, "it ain't going to happen." In the end it didn't, that distant war with its Imjin River disaster (shades of the Glorious Gloucesters), fizzling out just about where it began — and we were able to get on with our lives without that particular worry.

Once home from the escape of honeymoon, life slotted back into work mode for us, as we began to settle down to living in the familiar village of Hooe, where Mother had previously bought a cottage for us — a wonderfully generous action offering a base that needed only a peppercorn rent: a good start when money was tight. Maple Cottage was a perfect place to start a marriage, tiny, with low doorways (as I constantly found out), but with all the things we needed — plus resident good luck in the shape of a very black cat that moved in at about the same time as we did. Who could wish for more?

So with all that in the bag, we got down to another phase in our lives; Mary, delighted with our new home, did the housewife thing and forgot about hospitals — and I got my teeth into the business of running a farm and sorting out what to do with its staff of three workers and myself. It was a big change for both of us. I cycled the half-mile to the farm every morning at 7 a.m., set the men on to whatever needed doing, cycled back for breakfast — then returned to do what managers are paid for, which included pretty much everything. The farm was mainly arable, but ran a milking herd as well as bullocks for fattening down on the grazing land close to the marshes: it was a programme that kept me busy and I had to learn a lot, fast.

After we'd been settled in for a month or so, it was suggested to me by the local Home Guard Commander that I might like to rejoin — this time as a lieutenant, since my army service might make me useful. Having cleared it with Mary who was amused at the thought, doubtless thinking it would help keep me out of mischief, I was an army man again, more or less — but this time it was on my terms. I happily remembered Sergeant Jelly, his explosive wizardry and our lash-up drainpipe mortars from our Home Guard Sunday mornings long ago, fun times. I could handle that again — and did. Sadly, this renewed interest didn't last very long — as inevitably, like all good things, the time came when Dad's Army was disbanded; the war was done with, and expense would have been a big factor in government deliberations at a time when the country wasn't far off bankruptcy. Let me say with certainty, that the real Home Guard was a very different proposition from Captain Mainwaring's outfit at Walmington-on-Sea, and had it come to the crunch, it would have given a very good account of itself. The end of the Home Guard must have been a sad blow to many of those who had manned its ranks for so many years when the country most needed them — six years home-guarding would have left a big hole to fill.

Living and working in Hooe without its smugglers (obvious ones anyway) — but with laid-back neighbours, a pub that pulled such a lovely pint, its garage and shop that sold everything, was just the place to be; comfortably close to my old stamping grounds in Bexhill, it also had the strategic advantage of being near enough to Eastbourne for us to keep in touch with our respective parents, without being too close, a situation good for everybody, I'm sure. All things considered, they were gentle days in which to find our feet as a married couple.

Mary was the best thing that could have happened to me, being hugely influential in getting me round to being a normal human again. She was an "old soul" as a friend of ours once remarked, someone who must have been here before — or is miraculously aware of what usually takes a lifetime for most people to learn. She was the sensible one in the subtle ways that don't upset husbands — but balanced things by doing an occasional awful, like leaving our little piece of rationed Sunday joint in the oven and remembering only when we were miles away. But we didn't care, feasting on cornflakes instead; even as late as 1951 some food was still rationed, including bread for the first time, since apparently it didn't matter so much about national morale then.

We had fun, made love a lot, broke down in the ancient MG at weekends, and did what young married couples do. Very occasionally we could afford to have dinner and a dance at our favourite hotel in Eastbourne as a treat, and afterwards we'd go down to the beach a few yards away and paddle with my monkey-suit trousers rolled up, and Mary's long dress hoicked up to her knees. It was fabulous. Eastbourne Corporation had made a big postwar thing of planting its seafront gardens with myriad plants and flowers, and the air was heavy with night-scented stocks and other fragrances: all that — and a warm summer sea sucking and pulling at our feet amounted to something close to happiness. Damp and half-drunk with it all, we'd drive back across the empty marshes for what was left of Saturday night, with Sunday to come. For me, the world had settled.

Also available in ISIS Large Print:

Suburban Boy

Adrian Bristow

"It was while we lived in Herbert Road that I acquired my toy box . . . It was quite large enough for me to climb into and it became by turns a boat, a cave or a house, according to which story or character was exercising my imagination at the time."

Suburban Boy is the charming story of a bygone era, of a boy who grew up in south-east London in the 1930s. Adrian Bristow came from that great unsung mass — the lower middle-class. He grew up in the years before the war, which saw the Depression, the Abdication, the rise of Hitler and the coming of war. It was also a time of rising standards of living, burgeoning home ownership, social mobility and the emergence of first-generation graduates. It was a time when there was respect for authority and a strong consciousness of nation and empire.

ISBN 978-0-7531-9538-3 (hb)
ISBN 978-0-7531-9539-0 (pb)

In the Shelter of Each Other

Jack Maddox

"I prattled away and enthused and extolled the wonders of the library and this new experience all the way home. It changed my life, for it was a new interest with an infinite capability for progression and pleasure."

Liverpool, April 1932. England is out of work. The mills are silent, and in the river, ships are rusting at anchor. The king is ageing and his successor remains unmarried. In Germany Adolf Hitler has come to power and begun reclaiming lost territories.

It is the wrong time and place to arrive in the world, but Jack appears all the same. A childhood spent in a bustling dockside pub in the roughest, toughest part of the city and an early introduction to the school of hard knocks. Lawless, tribal and violent, but also exciting, humorous and generous. Bonded by poverty, few had much, but nobody died alone.

ISBN 978-0-7531-9536-9 (hb)
ISBN 978-0-7531-9537-6 (pb)